1 MONTH OF
FREE
READING

at

www.ForgottenBooks.com

By purchasing this book you are eligible for one month membership to ForgottenBooks.com, giving you unlimited access to our entire collection of over 1,000,000 titles via our web site and mobile apps.

To claim your free month visit:

www.forgottenbooks.com/free786665

ISBN 978-0-428-98074-0
PIBN 10786665

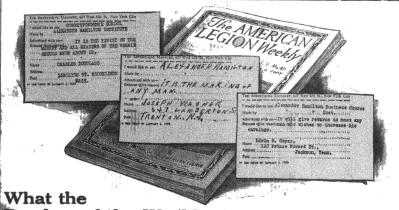

What the
Readers of the Weekly
Say about the Alexander Hamilton Institute

Read their testimony. Then find out about
this Modern Business Course and Service

MR. CUSHING, the Advertising Manager of THE AMERICAN LEGION WEEKLY, who is, by the way, a subscriber in the Alexander Hamilton Institute, asked you readers of the WEEKLY to tell him the American business organizations that should advertise in the WEEKLY and why. He asked you to fill in and sign a special coupon, giving the name of some national advertiser and the reasons why you thought their message should appeal to all Legion men.

* * *

Forty-six of the coupons returned to Mr. Cushing called for some advertising of the Alexander Hamilton Institute and 46 very good reasons were presented why we should use the advertising pages of the WEEKLY to advantage. Those 46 replies did more than give good selling ammunition to the advertising department of the WEEKLY. They also presented some very impressive indorsements of the value of the Institute's Modern Business Course and Service.

The answers came from every section of the country; in the

center of this page you will find representative comments from ten different men.

"I had always intended sending for 'Forging Ahead in Business' "

From Omaha a reader of the WEEKLY wrote at length:

"I had always intended sending for 'Forging Ahead in Business,' mentioned in the advertising of the Alexander Hamilton Institute in almost every leading magazine," he said. "But not until I saw the advertisement in the WEEKLY did I read *and act*. I am now glad to count myself one of their students and boosters."

Perhaps you, too, have been familiar with the main facts about the Institute. You know that behind it are men who represent the finest leadership in business, education and finance.

You know what it has done for thousands of other men, in every kind of business. You, too, have meant some time to send for "Forging Ahead in Business," that guide book of 116 pages which has proved so stimulating to so many other men.

* ** *

Only one moment of decision is required to place a copy in your hands. Will you act now, as these friends of yours have acted, by filling in the coupon and mailing it today? A copy is ready for you.

Alexander Hamilton Institute
893 Astor Place, New York City

Send me "Forging Ahead in Business" which I may keep without obligation

Name_____
Print here

Business
Address_____

Business
Position_____

Copyright 1920, Alexander Hamilton Institute

THE MOGUL OF THE PRESS ROOM

One of the Magazine Web Presses of WILLIAM GREEN, NEW YORK, Printers of THE AMERICAN LEGION WEEKLY

FIFTY TONS of paper are fed into this great press each week to produce THE AMERICAN LEGION WEEKLY.

Finished copies are delivered printed, folded and bound—at the rate of 24,000 an hour.

Then comes the big job of individually addressing, sorting, packing and mailing the 800,000 and more copies.

All this is done in remarkably short time—little more than a week from editorial rooms to reader.

Perhaps you have not been impressed with THE AMERICAN LEGION WEEKLY as "a thing of beauty." But the *quality is there*—editorially and mechanically—and when the price of paper drops, so that you can afford to use a better quality, your publication will equal any in the country.

We are proud of THE AMERICAN LEGION WEEKLY and of our part in its record-breaking accomplishments. We believe that The American Legion may well be proud of its publication. It's *your* paper to back and boost, but we're with you *strong*.

P.S. Most folks know of our big printing plant and our reputation for quality and service. We want them to know, too, of our EDITORIAL AND PLAN DEPARTMENT where we plan and build resultful catalogs and direct-by-mail advertising campaigns that, because they are based on experience, *produce results*.

WILLIAM GREEN · NEW YORK CITY

a Corporation

The AMERICAN LEGION Weekly

Official Publication of **The American Legion**

627 West Forty-third Street, New York City

OWNED EXCLUSIVELY BY THE AMERICAN LEGION

From the Retiring National Commander

To the Delegates at Cleveland and to All Legionnaires:

IT is but eighteen months since a few hundred American soldiers met at Paris and brought forth the idea of The American Legion. It is but ten months since, at Minneapolis, that idea was crystalized, committed to paper and made imperishable in the constitution of this organization.

The last ten months, like the eight that preceded them, have been crowded and eventful in the life of the Legion. They have seen it continue its growth with the spontaneity which marked its birth. They have seen it become a great organization, carrying its doctrines and policies into every city and town in this land and into other lands. They have seen it test and learn its power. They have seen this country come to look upon it as the highest exemplification of patriotism and citizenship.

The convention at Minneapolis left to each of the officers of the Legion, local, departmental and national, a vast amount of work and responsibility. Ours was the job of completing the task of organization, of perfecting the machinery to co-ordinate the Legion's efforts and to carry out its purposes and policies. Ours also was the job of executing a comprehensive program of accomplishment.

It was not an easy job. There was no precedent to guide us. Never before had there been an organization like this. There was a heavy burden of responsibility in the interpretation of the constitution and by-laws, in the formulation of rules and methods of procedure, and in making decisions to meet situations which the convention could not foresee. That the Legion has succeeded, that it has come to fulfill the expectations of the men who visualized it eighteen months ago, is due to the wonderful spirit of service to our country and our comrades evinced by the entire membership and to the unselfish leadership and untiring work of its local and departmental officers.

Speaking for the staff of National Headquarters —the men who have been associated with me during these last ten months—I can only say that they have worked hard and conscientiously. At all times it has been our policy to submerge our personal viewpoint in that of the Legion. We have carried out the work outlined by the last national convention to the best of our ability. Likewise have we met unforeseen situations, made decisions and executed them. Always, however, we have refrained, whenever possible, from making decisions

and establishing precedents which would affect the whole life of the Legion. The making of these decisions, we have felt, is for the Legion itself, as represented in its national convention.

This second annual convention at Cleveland finds The American Legion an organization which already has behind it a creditable record of accomplishment. We can review with satisfaction what we have done in our infancy for the disabled, for all ex-service men and for our country. It finds it also an organization which realizes that it has heavy obligations and much more to do in the future.

In many respects this convention is of extreme importance. Decisions are to be made which will affect the whole future of the Legion, which will, in a large measure, determine the usefulness of the organization for the rest of its existence. The delegates will have behind them, however, what the delegates at previous meetings did not have, a year's practical experience, with many lessons learned, with less uncertainty as to the wisdom of measures to be adopted or avoided. With implicit confidence can we leave the future of the Legion in their hands.

To attain the highest measure of success we must make use of two strong inherent American characteristics—common sense and tolerance. More and more must the Legion be the friendly meeting place of Americans of diverse but sincere opinions. The West, the East, the South, the North must continue to unite in our membership to exchange ideas and transmit ideals. Of each member only this must be required—that he has served America, has faith in America, and cherishes her institutions.

This convention is one of those milestones to which we will all look back proudly. It is not a pause in our advance, but a starting-point for new progress. Tolerance, common sense—let these be our watchwords as we go forward. And that we may better serve our country and our comrades, let us continue to assure ourselves of sound and unselfish leadership on the part of our post, departmental and national officers.

Franklin D'Olier

Retiring National Commander

"Soldier's Mail"—
From Lexington to the Argonne
The Last Letters Home of Four Americans, Representing Three Generations of One Family and Three Wars

THE B—— family of Massachusetts does not trace its New England antecedents back to the *Mayflower*, but it does rightly claim that its forebears came over in one of the earliest convoys. At least the family goes back to that period in American history when every able-bodied male carried a blunderbuss, when every cornfield might be converted on an instant's notice into a front-line trench and every hearthstone into a strongpoint.

The B—— family records do not regard those early days as "wartime." Life in Massachusetts then was too entirely a state of suspended or active hostilities to make it necessary to draw fine distinctions between war and peace.

But treasured in the B—— archives are four intensely human documents of other wars—of the three greatest wars in which American blood was ever shed. The documents are letters from four members of the B—— family, one a soldier in the American Revolution, one in the Civil War, and two in the World War. The letter in each case represents the last word of the man in uniform, were it Continental or Union blue or 1918 olive drab. For all four soldiers were killed in action, died of wounds or died of disease within a few days after writing what proved to be their farewell messages.

The first letter was written from a Continental camp at Roxbury, Massachusetts, just outside Boston, which was then in British hands. It must be remembered that spelling in those days was not one of the fine arts, that the wealthy Boston merchant with a dozen ships away to Jamaica for cargoes of rum, and the backwoods farmer, alike wrote in their own way, and that either was as likely to be right as the other. The letter follows:

Roxbury, December the 24, 1775.

Loven wife after my love and tender regards to you and the rest of my family. Hopen these Lines will find you as well as threw the great goodness of god they Leave me at this time.

I have no news to Right you the cannon play on our army every day but they hant plaid on Roxbery any sense we com down hear but they drove out the man of war out of the Harbor this day week and they wounded too of our meñ and that is all they have don by firen Last week. Western men are all well at present and I hop that they will Remain so there is nothing Strange to camps that has happened to us.

I should be glad that you wold take as good car of the catle as you can I mit have charge you first to take care of your Selves and as you have money by bred where you can git it and Dont Slip any oppertunity for that artakle Bread, for as wee hant but won Life to Live So let us Live today as tho wee new that we wase to dy tomoro my dear Children I would have them remember you Crater in the days of your youth indever as much as in you Lize to obay all god commandments in' So Doing you will obay your parence.

So I pray god to Direct you in all your ways and protect, you threw your youthfull days and keep you in his Richus ways So I Subscribe mySelf your Loven husban and to my children your tender and afathunat father.

E. B.

THE striking fact about the above letter is the omission of any reference to Christmas, despite its having been written on December 24. Christmas in those days was regarded as an unhallowed Popish invention, and its observance as a feast day was frowned on by the remnants of the Puritan theocracy, whose traditions were still all-powerful.

E. B. died of fever in Roxbury camp a few days after this letter was written. He had left his farm and his large family the day after the battle of Lexington, eight months before, and very probably fought at Bunker Hill.

The author of the second letter—the Civil War letter—was a boy of nineteen, and a rookie of the first water. He wrote:

Washington, Sept. 5th, 1862.
Dear Sister Carrie:

As I have nothing else to do, and thinking that you would like to hear from me I thought I would write and let you know how I am getting along. We are encamped now about 10 miles from Washington. We came here last Monday and have not had any tents since we left Hartford, so you see we have to sleep on the ground, but the most of us have built cabbins of brush to keep off the dew.

When we got here Monday it rained all night, and some of us stood up around the fire and some of us laid down on one blanket and got another over us and went to sleep wet as though we had been in the pond. When I got up in the morning the sun rose in the west or it looked as though it did, but it looks right to me now.

We have not drawn a ration of potatoes for four days it is almost time to drill so I must go.

I have just returned from drill have drilled one hour and ½ and have got to be on dress parrade in 1½ hours. We went out on parade ½ hour sooner than they told us for so I did not get fairly to writing before I was called off, while on parrade there was one man in Co. D had a fit and was carried to the Hospital.

I can hardly realize that I am in Virginia but the Country does not look the same. It looks like war. There is hardly a spear of grass to be seen it is all troden under foot and the trees are cut down all around we are only about 10 or 12 miles from Bull run and can hear cannon from there, did yesterday. John Nichols came here yesterday and is here now his Reg't is encamped about 6 miles from here. Albert West was here yesterday he came horse back he is only about 5 or 6 miles off. He had his horse shot under him last Saturday and has got a new one now, he said he saw the boys in the 11th Reg. a few weeks ago. The Stafford boys were all well. There is no very sick men in our company. C. West is Complaining a little and one or two others that you do not know, the rest of our boys are tough and don't give way to trifles.

It is getting rather late and I must close so goodby. Please excuse all mistakes and bad writing for I have to write on my knapsack and lay on the ground.

Write soon.

J. W. B.

J. W. B. did not stay long in camp. With a mass of untrained troops, he was thrown into the maelstrom of Antietam and fell, badly wounded, on September 17, 1862. For two days he lay on the battlefield, receiving more wounds, before he was finally picked up. He died October 11, 1862.

The third soldier, born in the United States, went to Canada with his family before the outbreak of war in 1914, and enlisted in one of the early Canadian contingents. His letter follows:

Somewhere in France,
June 12, 1916.
My Dear Folks:

At last I have a little time for writing letters. Big things have happened since I wrote last. The Canadians have been through the most intense bombardment that has ever been put on, and have lost very heavily, as the papers will tell you.

Our battalion had two companies in the front line. On the morning of *(Continued on page 48)*

(Continued on page 48)

The Second A. E. F.

This Year's Anticipated Battlefield Tourist Rush Failed to Develop—and There Are Many Reasons Therefor

By Timothy Vane

Dugout life these days has all the ingrained placidity of French rural existence hundreds of kilometers back from the old front-line

THERE is an idea in this country that the battlefields of France—and especially those of the Marne, the Argonne and St. Mihiel—are fairly swarming with American tourists. It isn't true. There is a notion that smartly dressed men and women fall over each other in a rush to inspect each remaining 'shell-hole and sustain an occasional casualty tumbling down the old dugout stairs; that large, larcenous hotels have sprung up near such eternal shrines as Rheims and Montfaucon, that the slightest halt in the traffic on the La Ferté or Varennes road immediately creates a string of fuming sight-seeing buses as long and indignant, if not as profane, as the queue of cussing trucks which used to block these roads two years ago. There is this notion. But it is a delusion.

It is true there have been Americans hurrying to Europe this summer in numbers sufficient to constitute almost a second A. E. F. Certainly by September there were more of us over there than there were when the old First Division slid into the sector northwest of Toul. Every boat that has put out from New York has been loaded like a transport with Europe-bound, passport-laden passengers.

The wildest prices have been asked (and paid) for berths and meals of a quality at which most sea-going Americans would have scoffed before

the war. As for any man who had bought a cabin and then decided at the last minute not to use it, he could sell his reservation at a sufficient profit to himself to enable him to buy a fine, modern, twelve-room house in the country and retire to it for the rest of his life. Ever since the first warm days of spring, there has been a stampede to Europe all right. But it has been no stampede to the battlefields. Many of the travelers have not been near them. Probably most of them have not.

THERE are a good many reasons for this. In the first place many of the voyagers are business men, going over as such. They are in a hurry. They have just ten days between the time when they dock at Southampton and the time when they must catch the homebound boat at Boulogne. They have nine appointments in London. They have three men to see in Paris. This last takes at least a week. It leaves them perhaps one free Sunday afternoon, which they proceed to blow on the races at Longchamps, and gives them time to see just as much devastation as can be glimpsed through the compartment window (tightly sealed)

as the train wheezes through Amiens on its way to the port.

Then of the more leisurely travelers, many are the old habitués of Europe who had been going over every year until 'the war put an inconvenient end to an agreeable custom. Now once more the ocean lanes are free of submarines and the ocean liners back at their old game of charging for the privilege, with nothing more to show for their transport days than many new tricks of making two passengers sleep where only one slept before. So the cosmopolites are traipsing over to their old haunts, motoring down shady Surrey roads, visiting the English lakes, mooning from château to château in rich Touraine, and winding up at the Swiss consulate in Paris, there to seek passport visas for Geneva and Lucerne. This last phase of their activity is a matter of intense exasperation to the French government officials, who never have been able to get it into American heads that the highest (and some of the loveliest) parts of the Alps are not in Switzerland at all, but in France.

These experienced travelers, who know just where the mellowest wines are cellared and just what unsuspected village in France boasts the finest cooks, are more interested this year in finding how many of their old haunts have been left unimpaired by the war than they are in surveying the great, silent stretches of devastation, in gazing at the still twisted trees of Belleau Wood or the house-stumps of Verdun. They know that the richer food, the more comfortable hotels, and the smoother roads—above all, the better roads—invite them to the parts of France unscorched by the war. Besides, many of the smartest and richest of them are from South America, and never were wildly interested in the war anyway.

THEN, in the mind of many an American whom the summer or fall may find in Paris within such easy distance of the great scenes, it must be admitted there is an unanalyzed and often unconscious, but none the less real and determining desire to forget the war—or let us say a desire not to be reminded of it. Perhaps he is one who served in the Army back home and

A demobilised poilu sets his house in order from the rubble of a wrecked village, and caps it with a tar-paper roof

of whom the still-smashed bridge at Château-Thierry would be a reminder of the greatest disappointment of his life. Perhaps he is one who was too old to serve, and whom the magazines and newspapers so saturated with the war at the time that he long ago reached the point where he could hold no more. Perhaps he is one who evaded service, who, deep in his heart, wishes to Heaven he hadn't, and to whom each blasted tree, each crumbled home, would point a finger, and at whom each murmur of rebuilding France, each clink of a hammer and whirr of a saw, would be a voice of stinging reproach. So he, too, goes to the Swiss consulate and hurries on.

But, you say, what of the returning men of the A. E. F.—don't they all want to go back over the old ground? Well, no, not all of them. They think they do, till they hit an M. P.-less Paris and then—and then—well, the thought of traveling a sacred road in a rubber-neck wagon or the thought of hiking alone to a well-remembered village without any of the old gang at hand to say: "Don't you remember when—" either thought is a dismayingone. So they slip into a seat at some café on the Boulevard des Italiens, order a coffee and cognac, and drowsily watch the world go strolling by. Then they go back over the battlefields—in memory.

Of the folk who do actually go to the battlefields, there are several classes. First among them are the fathers and mothers with graves to visit at Romagne, or at any of the several austere little cemeteries which mark the land, from the edge of Belleau Wood to the side of the railway track that passes by Juvigny. They are all that your best dreams of them would describe, these graveyards of the A. E. F., so pure, so plain, so silent, row on row of ungraded crosses, looking in the moonlight like some ghostly legion drawn up for the Last Inspection.

AND the fathers and mothers—somehow you recognize them even in the Place de l'Opéra in Paris, by the look in their faces, by their very quality as human beings. They may not wear black. They may even be laughing as they pass you by in the street. But you know them.

As it happens, there were many of these pilgrim mothers in the cabin list of the boat on which Elsie Janis crossed to England this summer. Instinct told her this when it came her turn in the program of the ship's concert, and she suggested that all hands join in singing a song she and her gang had often sung together in France. She started forth bravely, and soon a lot of quavering voices took up the melody. It was "There's a Long, Long Trail

A-Winding." She didn't finish it. No one did. It was probably the first instance of a ship's concert breaking up in tears.

I try to write lightly of these tourists, but somehow I keep remembering dusk at the edge of an American battlefield graveyard. A car is waiting in the road outside. The weary chauffeur, the father and the mother are searching up and down the rows of sentinel crosses. Somehow, they have become confused

in the directions given them from the neat card-catalogue of dead that is kept so efficiently in Paris.

Dark has overtaken them in their quest, and they must needs bend low over each cross and strain their eyes to read its name. The chauffeur is impatient to put his car up for the night. The father counsels their going on to Soissons for the night and resuming the search in the morning. "Come, Mamma," he says gently, "you're all tuckered out, and you'll be fresh and strong for it in the morning." But the mother, who has come from the other end of the world, feels she is too near the end of her quest to give in now or let another night of dreams come in between. So she stumbles along row on row, and then suddenly she stops. They see her bend low, bend lower, push back her veil the better to read the name before her. Then the quiet of descending night is torn by a woman's cry, a cry never to be forgotten.

I TRY to write good-humoredly of the tourists, and then I remember a day when some relief workers—members of the C. A. R. D. (Comité Américain pour les Régions Devastés)—were toiling in their bureau, when in bounced six rambunctious girls from the States, of whom the leader gushed as follows:

"We just stopped in to say we think your work is simply great and perfectly fascinating. We all lost our brothers in the war, and now we're seeing the sights. Well, we must run now. Olive oil."

I even try to write respectfully of the tourists, and then I remember the snickering that goes on in a certain village northeast of Soissons when the natives look up from their work long enough to watch the great twenty-seated automobiles go booming by. They noticed for a time that these cars, or some of them, drove boldly toward the famous Chemin-des-Dames, but always, at a point still some five or six kilometers from the real scene, turned off toward Fismes and Rheims, because the road up to the real battlefield was too bad for comfortable riding. Apparently the guide would wave vaguely over the landscape and shout: "There, ladies and gentlemen, is the famous Chemin - des - Dames." But it seemed rather a short-weight thrill to give folk who had paid good money and come all the way from Paris.

Then, after a time, the natives noticed that these cars did not push past the point of turning, but halted while all the people piled out and disappeared into the bowels of the earth, from which they later emerged thrilled to the core. The puzzled natives knew there had been no cave or quarry just there, and eventually went over to explore. They found, at a convenient distance from the crossroads, fortunately placed so that the cars could reach it before the driving became difficult, a great dugout, heavily shored with lumber and strewn with helmets and bits of old gas-masks, left lying there just as they might have been dropped when the Armistice was signed. It interested the natives mightily, this dug-out, because none of them remembered having seen it there before.

I try to write fondly of these sightseers, and then I remember a woman on the boat coming home, who was all of a flutter because she didn't know what her husband would say in his declaration to the Custom House about a certain trophy they were proudly bringing home as a gift to a friend of theirs—a dentist. The gift was a carefully polished human jaw-bone. They had picked it up on a field by the Ourcq.

IT was for such as these that the great tourist agencies, the automobile companies in Paris and Brussels, and many a guide, prepared their cars and their maps and their booklets this year, only to find that the traffic was less than half their expectations. The real pilgrims of the old A. E. F.
(Continued on page 42).

MEUSE–ARGONNE

September 26–November 11, 1918

Two years ago today an American army was deploying in the devastated region near Verdun to initiate the decisive battle of the World War. The task and the ordeal confronting our soldiers exceeded all past experiences in our history. The fate of the world hung in the balance. Through forty-seven days they maintained the battle until the enemy was completely defeated. To the fortitude, gallantry and devoted patriotism of those men, we owe the victory. Our dead and broken wounded discharged in full their duty to mankind and left a greater obligation to the living. Let us celebrate this anniversary with renewed resolution to do our whole part as citizens of our great country.

John J. Pershing

I'll Say It's Music

By Steuart M. Emery
Illustrations by WALLGREN

There's lots of kinds of music on this pleasant, earthly ball,
  Some say there's even music in the spheres;
I've been around a tidy while, I must have harked to all,
  And only one of 'em enthralls my ears.
I hear Chopin with pleasure and Beethoven with a grin,
  I laugh in glee at Mendelssohn's "Spring Song,"
But grand pianos haven't got the music that is in
  A little pair of bones a-going strong.

"Rake 'em up and break 'em up,
Put 'em down and take 'em up,
Wake 'em up and shake 'em up—a dollar's on the floor!"

A hurdy-gurdy in the street on ancient, battered wheels
  Revives my fainting spirits if they droop,
A jazz band's wild and raucous din has something that
  appeals—
I cannot hear my neighbor eat his soup.
Orchestral concerts, also, get due justice from my pen,
  I'm fond of wedding bells upon the breeze,
But not a melody compares with that which greets me when
  I listen to the dulcet ivories.

"Rake 'em up and break 'em up,
Put 'em down and take 'em up,
Wake 'em up and shake 'em up—a dollar's on the floor!"

The strumming of a banjo tune can stir the dumb to sing,
  A ukelele calls to wander-dreams,
A mandolin in tinkling tones is very apt to bring
  Old, tender memories where moonlight gleams.
A violin can cause the tears to overflow their dike,
  A drum can speed the heartbeats in a trice,
Still, none of 'em can rouse me to unleashed emotion like
  The music in a bounding pair of dice.

"Rake 'em up and break 'em up,
Put 'em down and take 'em up,
Wake 'em up and shake 'em up—a dollar's on the floor!"

The old "Suwanee River" is most beautiful to heed,
  I really hate to hear the last verse stop,
And "Silver Threads Among the Gold" sounds excellent,
  indeed,
  Upon the stage or in the barber shop.
A good duet's delightful and a quartet's twice as fine,
  I love the chorus in the music shows,
However, for real harmony, the sort that is divine,
  I'll take the animated dominoes.

When the War Movie Comes Back

How About a Little "Reelism" Instead of the "Forward, My Brave Lads" Features of Yesteryear?

By John A. Level

Cartoon by HELFANT

A WORLD-FAMOUS moving picture producer has just made the prediction that the war film would do a come-back within the next four or five years. He was so sure of this, he stated, that he was garnering scenarios against the day when the doughboy would have seconds out of the dish of glory.

When these "over there" screen dramas do come back—and they will come back—let's hope we see the "reel" thing—including the old greasewagon, the line-up at the alleged pail of hot and sparkling water, with two hundred and fifty slum-satiated hopefuls trying to dip their eating irons; the pompous greaseball at the goldfish counter; the little cootie in his various and sundry maneuvers; the husky trench rat bathing in the flare of a Very light. Even the flash of a French bathtub during a period of tragic crisis might be used effectively for comedy contrast.

In running back over the war pictures that have so far appeared, we must admit that errors in our new art have not been confined alone to the battle-ground and its environs. Custard pies have gone amiss and showered down on innocent bystanders; the dog with a note in his mouth which would have saved the long-suffering heroine has dashed from the fixed course, lured by the smell of a weinie shop; the villain has entered a swinging door wearing a red necktie and come out with a natty bow.

A LL we have to do to find out how little many Americans know about the war as it really was up until the time the home boys first got the short end of the exchange system at Brest and inland, is to scrutinize some of the films rushed to print in the days when

Let's hope we see the "reel" thing, including the little code in his various and sundry maneuvers

the Crown Quince twitched a careful mustache. Even in 1916 our screen doughboys were hopping the cushions as if they were going out on a college cross-country run, manicured, shaved and powdered, bowed down by no pack, iron rations, extra water bottle, hand grenades, bombs, wire cutters, helmets, blouses, shovels, canteen cheeks, dog tags or gas masks. The unvanquished bucks of the celluloid always rush an opposite line at a brisk trot, firing continuously the while they look for a soft place to do a Brodie. A little thing like a machine gun had no place in the seven-reel thriller, and rain and mud were far from the madding crowd. Lives he who hath witnessed in the movies a downhearted buck running a lighted match deftly over the seams of his o. d. shirt? I'll say not.

In the fall of 1916, when the Yanks were crossing the Canadian border in increasing numbers and our first war books were horrifying the uninitiated, there appeared in a Los Angeles daily an appeal for one thousand "soldiers" to mingle in a bloodless battle for the enlightenment of the hundred million. The picture was to portray the fall of a great nation, whereas it later proved the fall of many shekels, a couple of directors and some financiers.

The pilgrims came from far and wide, all colors, creeds and classes, glutting up the street car lines, thirsting to get at the villain's throat, and eager to eat. They assembled in a sector in the quiet of the California hills, assured of a simoleon a day and flax to snooze in at night beneath the silvery southern moon.

The management, not the general, had planned to send the boys into the fray happy, and three pie wagons started in file across the field of battle toward the hungry combatants. Instead of awaiting the cafeteria-style service, the great uncleaned and unfed dashed at the supply train. In passing it may be truthfully said that the three drivers recovered later in a hospital.

AT dawn the next day the sun arose, as per usual, except in France, and glistened on the field of honor. The trenches were some four hundred yards apart, and No Man's Land was a veritable beehive of plated dynamite. The cameras were set—they were off! Over the sandbags and into the jaws of death. The director had casually mentioned along the trenchs that some of the attacking force just needs fall along the wayside, giving a kick to the battle that would livelong thereafter in the minds of the movie fans. Directors make mistakes even as newly-made noncoms. After a run of a few score yards the soldats began falling in droves.

Only one man staggered, midst shot and shell, the entire stance. The remainder of the force afterward contended that he was a riger. Complaints were lodged by man about the distance; others pointed to the fact that breakfast had been postponed until after the set-to, and all others merely admitted they were to lazy to fight for one smack a day unless it was a close-up battle. The soldiers struck for two beans a battle, and won after a powerful word-barrage.

The war proceeded. On the very next charge buttons were pressed and the dynamite in No Man's Land kicked up the turf. The many who had tumbled jumped to escape the shower of debris. The wounded sprinted for shelter, and the dead made an equally hurried exit out of the firing zone.

Thousands of dollars were sunk in trying to make the birds stay dead. The scenes were photographed many, many times, and on an extra reward encouraged the screen soldiers to play possum alongside a piece of dynamite controlled by an expert on the sidelines.

THE German dummies suffered beyond repair. When not blown up by shell they were stripped of clothing and shoes by the half-driven and down-and-out participants. Many a bo emerged from the encounter fitted out with the best suit of clothing he had worn since he took his feet from under the festive board at home.

Among the heroes were a couple of I. W. W.'s known in the field of action simply as I.'s. These two philosophy that is well wor In looks they both resembl in the old soap advertisem seen making a testimonial used the soap once thirty and had used none other had traveled afar; both trouble along their journ

One alleged that Frisco town in the world. Wh in the Golden Gate city a dishwashers' union, to longed. These beetles thirteen bones a week dishwashers of all other c he had tarried grabbed or eleven iron men per.

The other bird play Wyoming. In Sheridan, the gods of his fathers, yo schooner of beer for a fi greater in height and wi schooner on any other bar country. The two I.'s fin blows over the relative t two centers of population picked up and carried to stretchers. In the Battle o these two and a party wh rocket go off in his wing casualties.

THE artillery was ma of a National Guard neighboring city, reinforc company-owned guns, m Both wooden gats suffere during the heat of batt blown to smithereens—or dinary in warfare, but a the movies.

For the mind of stuff there and two airplanes. Eve action was set the planes the infantry skidded forth was freed. But the air to mount, even after the ported for action five t the breeze caught her, low and dropped a fire direct hit. She caught fir the troopers stopped the enough to watch the o and spoil the set.

Unlike the real Army extras were paid off dai cleaned up with the live left the surroundings good-by forever. When ti ing the night scenes the walked off the field beca was refused them.

All the battlers were perfect physical specimer ber with major handica examination and flung t the fray. All those who porarily buried alive in and a half, while those through a thick smoke vicinity of the planted out for double time. W was all wrong, the soldi act, retiring to the dres sending forth a spokes sisted on a new bill of f

Will the war movie o the one the big director come back—be this t travesty? There is good it will not. If it is, le beware. There will be experts in his audience to make themselves hear hero starts over the top in one hand and a swor

First Generation Heroes

Not a Few Medals of Honor Were Won Near the Spots Where Some of the A. E. F.'s Fighting Ancestors Had Carried On in Earlier Wars

By Philip Von Blon

is Cukela, whose Czech fighti d won him fame near Villers-Co ts, is still with the Marines, and s in Haiti helping maintain ord

Jake Allex, hero of Chipilly Ridge, is spending a vacation at his home town in Serbia before returning to his former job in a Chicago stockyards office

DURING the months when a America was rejoicing over th ending of the war and ever in the land was welcoming its r ing sons, the village of Nortran orway maintained its unruffled pl y. True, the momentous develo ts of Europe's readjustment we cted in the discussions of the No an newspapers and figured in th at the inns, and every villager wh rned from a voyage to the la gerent countries was called upo ll what he had seen and heard. An ybody in the town hoped that price ld be lowered and that the greed ands of the hungry fighting nation ld end and food become more plentiful on home tables. But these were only echoes of the anxious days. Nortrand for the most part kept evenly at its accustomed tasks.

For a whole year the postman had been delivering strangely marked envelopes at the home of Thornlief Waaler. The envelopes did not bear postage stamps, but in a lower corner each one bore the blue-inked impression of a rubber stamp and undecipherable writing, all in a strange language. And the man who received them sometimes showed his neighbors parts of the letters where heavy blurs of ink had obliterated parts of the message. In several of the letters whole lines had been snipped out by the scissors. The Norwegian householder made no secret of the fact that they came from the fighting front in France—from the American front—and evidences of the all-embracing censorship were not new to Norway.

Then one day Nortrand awakened to find that it had a real homecoming of a real war hero. The village had never forgotten Reidar Waaler, who, several years before, had left his father's home to become a trader in that fabled Bagdad on America's eastern shore, the city of New York, where men of all countries buy and sell things amid marvelous artificial surroundings. The boy who had lived among the hills that fall sheerly away to deep, silent fjords had been transplanted to a skyscraper.

And now he was back, with the mantle of heroism upon him. The letters he had sent from France had told something of a hard fight, but it was not until the sturdy, light-haired young man, standing beside the hearth he had known as a boy, had shown the medal and ribbon he had received for his part in that fight, that the town knew that it had produced for America one of its greatest heroes of the war.

For that medal was the Congressional Medal of Honor, and Reidar Waaler was one of only fifty-four American soldiers who had received it for supreme gallantry, and had lived to wear it.

THE medal recalled a deadly hour on the Hindenburg line at Ronssoy on the day that the Americans and British launched their combined attack, which was one phase of the beginning of the end of the war. In that hour Sergeant Waaler, of the 105th Machine Gun Battalion of the Twenty-seventh Division, had crawled forward under heavy enemy fire to a burning British tank. He had rescued two wounded men and carried them to safety. He had then returned to the tank and searched until he was sure none of the others in the tank crew were alive. His act was an epic of supreme unselfishness.

After the Armistice, Waaler became manager of the New York office of an import and export house doing business with Scandinavian countries, and his

ar Waaler, one of the fifty-four est living American heroes, was in Norway, and is now in the dinavian import and export trade

Louis Van Iersal, born in Holland, won the Medal of Honor by swimming the Meuse under close enemy fire. He is now a bank watchman at Passaic, N. J.

Let's hope we see the "reel" thing, including the little cootie in his various and sundry maneuvers

the Crown Quince twitched a careful mustache. Even in 1916 our screen doughboys were hopping the cushions as if they were going out on a college cross-country run, manicured, shaved and powdered, bowed down by no pack, iron rations, extra water bottle, hand grenades, bombs, wire cutters, helmets, blouses, shovels, canteen checks, dog tags or gas masks. The unvanquished bucks of the celluloid always rush an opposite line at a brisk trot, firing continuously the while they look for a soft place to do a Brodie. A little thing like a machine gun had no place in the seven-reel thriller; and rain and mud were far from the madding crowd. Lives he who hath witnessed in the movies a downhearted buck running a lighted match deftly over the seams of his o. d. shirt? I'll say not.

In the fall of 1916, when the Yanks were crossing the Canadian border in increasing numbers and our first war books were horrifying the uninitiated, there appeared in a Los Angeles daily an appeal for one thousand "soldiers" to mingle in a bloodless battle for the enlightenment of the hundred million. The picture was to portray the fall of a great nation, whereas it later proved the fall of many shekels, a couple of directors and some financiers.

The pilgrims came from far and wide, all colors, creeds and classes, glutting up the street car lines, thirsting to get at the villain's throat, and eager to eat. They assembled in a sector in the quiet of the California hills, assured of a simoleon a day and flax to snooze in at night beneath the silvery southern moon.

The management, not the general, had planned to send the boys into the fray happy, and three pie wagons started in file across the field of battle toward the hungry combatants. Instead of awaiting the cafeteria-style service, the great uncleaned and unfed dashed at the supply train. In passing it may be truthfully said that the three drivers recovered later in a hospital.

AT dawn the next day the sun arose, as per usual, except in France, and glistened on the field of honor. The trenches were some four hundred yards apart, and No Man's Land was a veritable beehive of planted dynamite. The cameras were set—they were off! Over the sandbags and into the jaws of death. The director had casually mentioned along the trenches that some of the attacking force must needs fall along the wayside, giving a kick to the battle that would live long thereafter in the minds of the movie fans. Directors make mistakes, even as newly-made noncoms. After a run of a few score yards the soldats began falling in droves.

Only one man staggered, midst shot and shell, the entire distance. The remainder of the force afterward contended that he was a ringer. Complaints were lodged by many about the distance; others pointed to the fact that breakfast had been postponed until after the set-to, and still others merely admitted they were too lazy to fight for one smack a day unless it was a close-up battle. The soldiers struck for two beans a battle, and won after a powerful word-barrage.

The war proceeded. On the very next charge buttons were pressed and the dynamite in No Man's Land kicked up the turf. The many who had tumbled jumped to escape the shower of debris. The wounded sprinted for shelter, and the dead made an equally hurried exit out of the firing zone.

Thousands of dollars were sunk in trying to make these birds stay dead. The scenes were photographed many, many times, and only an extra reward encouraged the screen soldiers to play possum alongside a piece of dynamite controlled by an expert on the sidelines.

THE German dummies suffered beyond repair. When not blown up by shell they were stripped of clothing and shoes by the hard-driven and down-and-out participants. Many a bo emerged from the encounter fitted out with the best suit of clothing he had worn since he took his feet from under the festive board at home.

Among the heroes were a couple of I. W. W.'s known on the field of action simply as I.'s. These two I.'s had a philosophy that is well worth repeating. In looks they both resembled the tramp in the old soap advertisement, who was seen making a testimonial "that he had used the soap once thirty years before and had used none other since." Both had traveled afar; both had stirred up trouble along their journey.

One alleged that Frisco was the best town in the world. Why? Because in the Golden Gate city there existed a dishwashers' union, to which he belonged. These beetles pulled down thirteen bones a week, whereas the dishwashers of all other cities in which he had tarried grabbed a measly ten or eleven iron men per.

The other bird played Sheridan, Wyoming. In Sheridan, he swore by the gods of his fathers, you could get a schooner of beer for a five-cent piece greater in height and width than any schooner on any other bar in any other country. The two I.'s finally came to blows over the relative merits of the two centers of population, both being picked up and carried to the rear on stretchers. In the Battle of Two Weeks these two and a party who let a smoke rocket go off in his wing were the only casualties.

THE artillery was made up mostly of a National Guard unit from a neighboring city, reinforced by two big company-owned guns, made of wood. Both wooden gats suffered direct hits during the heat of battle, and were blown to smithereens—rather extraordinary in warfare, but a knockout in the movies.

For thrill stuff there were a blimp and two airplanes. Every time the action was set the planes were signaled, the infantry skidded forth and the blimp was freed. But the air-sack refused to mount, even after the planes had reported for action five times. Finally the breeze caught her, a plane soared low and dropped a firecracker for a direct hit. She caught fire, and some of the troopers stopped the battle long enough to watch the overhead action and spoil the set.

Unlike the real Army, these screen extras were paid off daily. Those who cleaned up with the ivories promptly left the surroundings, going AWOL and good-by forever. When it came to taking the night scenes the hired hands walked off the field because extra pay was refused them.

All the battlers were supposed to be perfect physical specimens, but a number with major handicaps got by the examination and flung themselves into the fray. All those who had to be temporarily buried alive insisted on time and a half, while those who dashed through a thick smoke screen in the vicinity of the planted dynamite hung out for double time. When the stuff was all wrong, the soldiers refused to act, retiring to the dressing-rooms and sending forth a spokesman who insisted on a new bill of fare.

Will the war movie of the future—the one the big director is sure will come back—be this type of battle travesty? There is good reason to think it will not. If it is, let the producer beware. There will be a whole lot of experts in his audience who are going to make themselves heard as soon as the hero starts over the top with the colors in one hand and a sword in the other.

First Generation Heroes

Not a Few Medals of Honor Were Won Near the Spots Where Some of the A. E. F.'s Fighting Ancestors Had Carried On in Earlier Wars

By Philip Von Blon

Louis Cukela, whose Czech fighting blood won him fame near Villers-Cot-terets, is still with the Marines, and is now in Haiti helping maintain order

Jake Allex, hero of Chipilly Ridge, is spending a vacation at his home town in Serbia before returning to his former job in a Chicago stockyards office

DURING the months when all America was rejoicing over the ending of the war and every town in the land was welcoming its returning sons, the village of Nortrand in Norway maintained its unruffled placidity. True, the momentous developments of Europe's readjustment were reflected in the discussions of the Norwegian newspapers and figured in the talk at the inns, and every villager who returned from a voyage to the late belligerent countries was called upon to tell what he had seen and heard. And everybody in the town hoped that prices would be lowered and that the greedy demands of the hungry fighting nations would end and food become more plentiful on home tables. But these were only echoes of the anxious days. Nortrand for the most part kept evenly at its accustomed tasks.

For a whole year the postman had been delivering strangely marked envelopes at the home of Thornlief Waaler. The envelopes did not bear postage stamps, but in a lower corner each one bore the blue-inked impression of a rubber stamp and undecipherable writing, all in a strange language. And the man who received them sometimes showed his neighbors parts of the letters where heavy blurs of ink had obliterated parts of the message. In several of the letters whole lines had been snipped out by the scissors. The Norwegian householder made no secret of the fact that they came from the fighting front in France—from the American front—and evidences of the all-embracing censorship were not new to Norway.

Then one day Nortrand awakened to find that it had a real homecoming of a real war hero. The village had never forgotten Reidar Waaler, who, several years before, had left his father's home to become a trader in that fabled Bagdad on America's eastern shore, the city of New York, where men of all countries buy and sell things amid marvelous artificial surroundings. The boy who had lived among the hills that fall sheerly away to deep, silent fjords had been transplanted to a skyscraper.

And now he was back, with the mantle of heroism upon him. The letters he had sent from France had told something of a hard fight, but it was not until the sturdy, light-haired young man, standing beside the hearth he had known as a boy, had shown the medal and ribbon he had received for his part in that fight, that the town knew that it had produced for America one of its greatest heroes of the war.

For that medal was the Congressional Medal of Honor, and Reidar Waaler was one of only fifty-four American soldiers who had received it for supreme gallantry, and had lived to wear it.

THE medal recalled a deadly hour on the Hindenburg line at Ronssoy on the day that the Americans and British launched their combined attack, which was one phase of the beginning of the end of the war. In that hour Sergeant Waaler, of the 105th Machine Gun Battalion of the Twenty-seventh Division, had crawled forward under heavy enemy fire to a burning British tank. He had rescued two wounded men and carried them to safety. He had then returned to the tank and searched until he was sure none of the others in the tank crew were alive. His act was an epic of supreme unselfishness.

After the Armistice, Waaler became manager of the New York office of an import and export house doing business with Scandinavian countries, and his

Reidar Waaler, one of the fifty-four greatest living American heroes, was born in Norway, and is now in the Scandinavian import and export trade

Louis Van Iersal, born in Holland, won the Medal of Honor by swimming the Meuse under close enemy fire. He is now a bank watchman at Passaic, N. J.

return to his old home was a part of a trade tour through Norway, Sweden and Denmark. He and his bride are starting this week on a honeymoon voyage to his boyhood home.

WAALER is not the only Medal of Honor man who was born in Europe. The record of the whole seventy-eight awards of the medal show that first generation Americans figured conspicuously in heroism in proportion to their numbers on the roll of the A. E. F. And the names of the men who appear on that roll illustrate the truth that America's Army in France was composed of men sprung from all of Europe's races, even though the majority of them, of course, were "later generation" Americans. The Army was the proof of the perfect fusion of all people which had made America great peacefully, of the fact that this nation has created a homogeneous citizenship of undivided loyalty out of so many different elements which had come to her from across the sea.

Jake Allex, formerly of the 131st Infantry, Thirty-third Division, who won the Medal of Honor at Chipilly Ridge by leading a platoon after all its officers had been killed, and personally advanced thirty yards in the face of intense fire, killed five of the enemy with his bayonet and, using his gun as a club, captured fifteen prisoners, had to go all the way from Chicago to Serbia to get a homecoming welcoming in his native town. Incidentally, his triumphal journey was made possible by the fact that his old employers, Morris & Company, Chicago meat packers, gave him a vacation and $3,000 for expenses. He is still in Serbia, but some day he will be back at his old job in the stock yards.

LOUIS VAN IERSAL is day watchman at a bank in Passaic, N. J., but when he is sure there are no pickpockets or hold-up men about he probably dreams of dykes and windmills and brilliant tulip fields. For his birthplace is Dussen, Holland.

Few of the incidents of the war are more thrilling than the story of this bank watchman's big deed. At Mouzon, on the Meuse, two days before the Armistice, Van Iersal's regiment, the Ninth Infantry of the Second Division, was prevented from advancing by deadly enemy fire. A half-wrecked bridge spanned the river between the American advance guard and the enemy. Van Iersal volunteered to cross the bridge and reconnoitre. He started out under machine gun and rifle fire from the Germans, who were less than seventy-five yards distant. Half-way across the bridge he came upon a trap. A section of the bridge gave way and he tumbled into the water. While American watchers believed he had been killed, he kept on swimming, despite a strong current, and finally reached the opposite shore. There he observed how the enemy was distributed for the defense of the bridge.

Then he swam back across the river.

And now—well, a bank watchman is most efficient when he is least conspicuous. The depositors take him for granted the same as they do the fixtures. He is as impersonal as the traffic policeman. The perspiring fat man who comes into the bank and finds lines standing in front of the tellers' windows may turn impatiently to the affable young man who stands near the entrance and ask him to send a message to an official behind the gratings. He would not know that he is addressing the hero of Mouzon on the Meuse. The Medal of Honor rosette in the lapel of the watchman's coat has no rating in the money market. But Louis Van Iersal knows that it stands for something in his own heart—the something that was a part of the will of the A. E. F., and gives to every hero a life heritage that is beyond the power of bank balances to buy.

LOUIS CUKELA won fame and the Medal of Honor in the Fifth Regiment of the Marine Corps near Villers-Cotterets at the beginning of the Second Division's historic thrust toward Soissons in mid-July of 1918, and by his deed a Czech name is emblazoned on the nation's record of her bravest men. Cukela, however, was born in Minnesota, and to him Bohemia is only a land of tradition.

The fighting instinct that had come down to him through generations of fighting ancestors in Europe showed itself on that July day in France when Sergeant Cukela crawled out alone toward an enemy position under heavy fire, disregarding the warning of his comrades. He succeeded in getting behind the German lines and rushed a machine gun emplacement, killing or driving off the enemy gunners with his bayonet. Then he used German hand grenades to bomb the enemy out of the adjoining portion of the offensive system and captured single-handed two machine guns and four prisoners.

Anyone seeking Cukela now will have to take a boat for Haiti. The sergeant of Villers-Cotterets is still in the Marine Corps, but he is a lieutenant.

THERE could be selected no handful of American heroes without at least one Irish name in it. The name of John J. Kelly, formerly of the Sixth Regiment of Ma-

(Continued on page 48)

TWO YEARS AGO
By Grantland Rice

Through the crowded streets where the arc lights burn,
Or perhaps apart from the toiling band,
Once in a while old dreams return
Of another life in another land:
Old dreams of bugles and marching men
Where a sergeant growls "Fall In" again.

The world drifts by as I watch once more
The doughboys slog through an old French town,
With its shattered walls that are red with gore,
Through its muddy streets as the rain beats down;
Their grim young faces—rifle and pack—
Hiking on to the next attack.

I see them now as the chow lines form;
Pal and buddy and fighting mate,
Ready again for the next day's storm
From the Hun barrage where the big guns wait;
Where the muffled roar through the flaming night
Has sent them word of the next day's fight.

Through St. Mihiel and the Argonne drifts,
Waiting word for the next advance,
As the mist rolls up and the gray fog lifts
I can see them now in the woods of France,
Knee-deep still in the muck and mire,
Working their way through the tangled wire.

Ghosts in khaki—they linger still
As each drifts by with the old platoon,
Holding a dugout on some hill
Where only machine gun bullets croon
In the last big drive through the maw of hell
That took Sedan as the curtain fell.

There's a long trail that is winding back
Through the battered towns with their mud and rain,
Where the world has forgotten both man and pack
In the older struggle for gold and gain;
The world has forgotten—but now and then
We dream that the bugle has blown again.

Is it only a dream when we hear once more
The caissons rumble across the hills?
When the howitzers bark with their ancient roar
In the life that carried a thousand thrills?
Only a dream for the fallen mate
Who sleeps where the wooden crosses wait!

The Service Record of the Legion

A Digest of Eighteen Months of Definite Accomplishment in the Interests of the Ex-service Man, His Community and His Country

A CIVILIZATION that moves so fast that it may no longer record its progress by the old figurative paintings of history, but must see its own unrolling past as the swiftly-changing pictures of the cinematographic film, finds in the growth of The American Legion a headliner on the program of modern times.

From its first flicker as an idealistic dream, down through eighteen months, the picture of the Legion's growth flashes on the screen of the present as a world-wide panoramic spectacle in which 2,000,000 men and fifty thousand women are seen marching forward, under a common banner of American nationalism to an inspiring destiny.

The flashes which come between the first and latest pictures record eighteen months of tremendous efforts and great accomplishments, and as the reel unfolds simultaneously with time the audience of America looks to the future for the fulfillment of the promise which it sees in the efforts of the vast army of veterans of the World War.

The spectators know that the plot of the future national drama is a complex one that will require successful acting on the part of the whole nation of 110,000,000 people, and, arguing from the past performances of the cohesive army of organized veterans, it knows that The American Legion will continue at the front and center of the national stage.

The future, of course, is unknown. But the last eighteen months of the picture have been run off, and their pictures—the record of the first eighteen months of The American Legion—may now be reviewed. It is the purpose of this review to select and describe some of those pictures, to show what The American Legion has already done, to show how important the organization has become in the daily life of the whole nation. The actual increase in membership is in itself an index of the accomplishments of The American Legion. At the close of the Minneapolis Convention, less than a year ago, the organization had approximately 4,000 posts, distrib-

The pages that follow are devoted to summarizing in brief space the accomplishments of The American Legion during the fiscal year that will end with the Second National Convention at Cleveland next week

uted through fifty Departments. On August 28 last, there were 9,709 posts in seventy departments. In nine and one-half months 5,700 new posts were organized. In the same period, also, 1,259 units of the Women's Auxiliary were formed.

THE new posts were organized and chartered at the rate of 150 a week, twenty-one a day—almost one an hour. To keep pace with this growth required the expansion and building-up of the early, rather loosely-knit mushroom growth of posts within the United States into a compact organization. The departments gradually forged ahead into full efficiency and, working with National Headquarters, established those necessary lines of communication which have made the organization homogeneous in spirit and action.

From the borders of the United States the organization had spread out to the corners of the world. In such widely separated lands as China and Poland, Argentine and Canada, the traveling Legionnaire from the United States may find himself among comrades. Forty-three posts of The American Legion are distributed through American possessions and foreign countries.

This growth has added significance from the fact that, both in the United States and abroad, new posts were formed without the assistance of national organizers, although in a few States, notably Illinois, Department representatives did notable missionary work in bringing new posts into existence.

At the close of the Minneapolis Convention, few Department headquarters were equipped for the administrative functions which they are now carrying, and a great share of the early burden of organization was born at National Headquarters. The extent of National Headquarters' whole task is indicated by figures showing that between November 13, 1919, and August 31, 1920, 112,448 letters, 4,238 packages and 4,303 telegrams were received at the Indianapolis offices, while in the same period 160,877 letters, 25,447 packages and 3,321 telegrams were dispatched.

On December 1, 1919, there were 29 persons at work in National Headquarters. In the following March, under pressure of new work, this number had increased to 51. At present the National Headquarters personnel includes forty persons, drawn from the States as follows: Connecticut, 1; Georgia, 1; Indiana, 23; Maine, 1; Minnesota, 2; Missouri, 1; New Mexico, 1; New York, 7; Pennsylvania, 1; Vermont, 1, and Washington, 1. Of the yearly budget of $150,000, allowed at the last National Convention for the operation of National Headquarters, a portion will be unexpended at the end of the fiscal year.

Only ten percent of national dues collected from members was made available for the operation of National Headquarters. The sale of more than 700,000 articles of merchandise, such as flags, insignia and similar articles, all valued at $320,000, has yielded profits which have gone far toward meeting expenses.

THE accomplishment in which The American Legion may take most justifiable pride is its special service rendered to all ex-service men and women, and particularly to the sick and disabled veterans and their dependents.

The American Legion realized from the start its obligation to assist all former soldiers and sailors to obtain settlements for any claims arising out of war service. Thousands of men, unacquainted with official formalities, returned to civil life without receiving Army pay due to them, without receiving the $60 bonus given on discharge and with their Army accounts relating to Liberty Bonds and War Risk Insurance badly tangled. Thousands of dependents of those service men who lost their lives had failed to obtain payments due them under War Risk Insurance. Many thousands of disabled and partly disabled veterans were struggling to readjust themselves in civilian life and proving a burden to their relatives, unaware of the procedure necessary to obtain financial assistance from the Government.

The American Legion attacked these problems energetically. At National Headquarters a Service Division was established, which kept in closest touch with all Government agencies and communicated all information to Departments and posts of the Legion. A great majority of the posts elected or appointed a special officer, often known as the War Risk Officer, who was charged with the duty of helping all veterans to obtain justice from Washington. In posts which did not select a special officer for this duty, the post commander or post adjutant rendered assistance.

In almost every community not only Legionnaires, but veterans generally, came to rely upon The American Legion as the agency through which they might obtain settlement of all their claims. The War and Treasury Departments gave special attention to claims submitted through Legion officials, and the handling of correspondence by these Legion officials who developed expert knowledge of insurance and compensation affairs tended to produce quick results.

IN many cities, posts carried on campaigns of education to acquaint veterans with their rights, and many men were reminded of the value of carrying their War Risk Insurance and of taking steps for medical examinations so that they might obtain Government treatment for slow-developing ailments resulting from their service.

The volume of assistance of this character rendered by the posts and Departments is incalculable. The Legion is still maintaining this service and is finding that, in spite of the time which has elapsed since the Armistice, thousands of new cases are being brought forward.

Directly related to these efforts as a whole are the special efforts made to help veterans entitled to hospital treatment and to rehabilitation training under the Federal Board for Vocational Education. These men, in great part, had a hard time fighting the battle of red tape. In the maze of Government regulations they often became confused to the point of despair, and many of them were abandoning efforts to obtain any help. It had been apparent for some time that amendments to the War Risk Insurance Act were being unduly delayed in the Senate, causing unnecessary want and privation among thousands of men and women for whom the measure should have provided.

Attention was focused on the inadequacy of official provisions for the disabled and their dependents when THE AMERICAN LEGION WEEKLY published an exposé of conditions and the press of the country followed up with verbal bombardments of the Bureau of

The Convention Program

Following is the tentative program which will be observed by the delegates to the Second Annual National Convention of The American Legion at Cleveland:

Monday, September 27

9 A.M. —Caucus of each Department Delegation at the Department Headquarters.

10 A.M. —The Convention is called to order.
Invocation by the National Chaplain.
Addresses of welcome.
Report of the National Commander.
Report of Executive Committee on Convention Program.
Naming of Convention Committees.
Announcement of time and place of committee meetings.
Report of the National Adjutant and the National Treasurer.
Reports of committees.

The afternoon and evening will be devoted to the parade and entertainment by the city of Cleveland. Members of committees will meet with their respective committees.

Tuesday, September 28

9 A.M. —The Convention assembles. Reports of committees.

Wednesday, September 29

9 A.M. —The Convention assembles.
Unfinished business.
New business.
Election of officers.
Adjournment.

Preliminary to the opening of the Convention, a meeting of all delegation secretaries will be held at The Hollenden at 10 A.M., Friday, September 24, when each secretary will receive all instructions, badges, tickets for entertainment, etc., necessary for his delegation. On Saturday, September 25, the National Executive Committee will meet at The Hollenden at 10 A.M., with old and new members and the chairmen of the delegations present.

The new Executive Committee will meet at 10 A.M. in The Hollenden on Thursday, September 30.

War Risk Insurance and the Federal Board for Vocational Education.

On December 15 the Legion concentrated its efforts to obtain action, and particularly the consolidation of the three Governmental agencies which deal with the disabled. On that day there was held in Washington a conference attended by the national officers of The American Legion and the department commanders of all the States or their representatives. R. G. Cholmeley-Jones, director of the War Risk Insurance Bureau, made all arrangements for holding the conference and provided transportation for the men who attended.

The conference considered the Sweet and the Wason Bills, then pending,

and made recommendations to Congress. Within forty-eight hours the Sweet Bill was passed by the Senate under suspension of the rules and without a roll call, the first time anything of the kind had occurred since the Civil War. The bill increased the monthly allowance for disabled men from $30 to $80 a month.

More recently, through efforts of The American Legion, Congress voted to increase the compensation for disabled men taking vocational training from $80 to $100 a month, in the case of veterans in city districts where the cost of living makes the $80 rate inadequate.

EQUALLY conspicuous success attended the efforts of The American Legion to induce the Federal Board for Vocational Education to change its old system of dealing with the disabled veterans from its central offices at Washington to a system under which representatives of the Federal Board are distributed through districts which cover the whole United States.

The former delays have been eliminated, for disabled men now may have personal contact with agents of the Board at convenient distances from their homes. Since the decentralization of the system, the work of enrolling the disabled has proceeded rapidly, until today between 40,000 and 50,000 are wards of the Board. The Departments and posts of The American Legion are working in close harmony with the Federal Board in seeing that each case is judged on its merits.

The Legion also has brought about revolutionary improvements in the system of providing hospital treatment for the veterans who still require it. In all parts of the country, posts and Departments have kept in close contact with the patients, often making a practice of having delegations visit the hospitals weekly to offer their services to the convalescents or the bedridden.

In certain sections, hospital accommodations proved unsuitable for the classes of patients assigned to them, and the Legion has succeeded in having men transferred to hospitals more adapted for their care or has brought about reforms in the hospitals. The continuing importance of this work of hospital supervision is emphasized by the increasing number of veterans who are being compelled to seek treatment for old wounds or ailments. Public health officials have estimated that it will be seven or eight years before the need for hospital accommodations for veterans decreases.

ASSISTING the wounded and disabled has been the first thought of The American Legion, but all the time it was rendering such assistance it has been engaged also in a country-wide movement to obtain just compensation for all veterans. It has appealed to Congress and the nation to equalize the financial sacrifices which the overwhelming majority of service men made by leaving homes and trades and businesses. It has argued that it is the nation's duty to compensate in some measure those who served in the Army or Navy with small pay, while men not called to the colors were profiting by the abnormal prosperity of war—

The latchstring is always out at the American Legion clubhouse in Cleveland, O. (right)

A three-story house (above) surrounded by shade trees is headquarters for the Pine Grove, Pa., Post

This ivy-clad house (left) shelters Henry H. Houston, 2d, Post, of Philadelphia

Low and rambling, the clubhouse of the Wilmington, N. C., Post (above) radiates Southern hospitality

The clubrooms of the Benjamin F. Haecker Post, of Eureka, Ill. (above) are a lure to festivity

Poppies from Flanders Fields have been planted in the yard of the home of the Charles P. Rowe Post (left), of Pomona, Cal.

time, piling up huge profits or drawing unusually high wages.

At the Minneapolis Convention, the Legion declared in unmistakable terms that it desired compensation for all veterans, but refrained, at that time, from making a definite request. It stated that it "left, with confidence, to the Congress, the discharge of this obligation."

THE Legislative Committee, conforming to this resolution, appeared before Congress and advocated the passage of some form of beneficial legislation. In February, however, it became apparent that the sentiment of Congress was apathetic, and to some extent hostile, toward any such legislation.

There was reason to suspect that, in the words of the National Commander, Franklin D'Olier, there was being made a deliberate attempt to "kiss adjusted compensation to death." Scores of bills had been introduced in both houses, involving many different principles of compensation and creating a situation as confusing as wily legislators could have been expected to make it. In addition, there was a difference of opinion as to the means of raising the money which boded ill for the prospects of the passage of any legislation.

On February 10, the National Executive Committee of the Legion met in Washington and started aggressive action to carry out the spirit of the Minneapolis Convention recommendation. The committee informed Congress that the Legion favored the payment of a $50 bond for each month of service to each person who had served in the Army, Navy or Marine Corps.

At another meeting of the National Executive Committee in Washington on March 22, 23, and 24, the Beneficial Legislation Committee recommended that the Legion center all its efforts for the adoption of the four-fold plan of beneficial legislation, which was later introduced in Congress as the Fordney Bill. Every State was represented at this meeting.

There was no difference of opinion over the first three features of the bill —providing aid to enable veterans to obtain farms, homes or vocational education, but several States opposed the

fourth option providing for cash compensation. On the final vote, however, all but eight States withdrew this opposition and joined in the endorsement of the four-fold legislation plan. Several Departments, notably Florida and South Carolina, among the smallest in point of membership, continue to oppose the cash option feature.

This four-fold plan is already embodied in a bill which has been adopted by the House of Representatives and is now pending in the Senate. The report of the National Legislative Committee, appearing elsewhere in this issue, covers in more detail the Legion's effort to obtain passage of the bill. The results achieved so far have only been possible through the joint work of Legionnaires throughout the United States in letting the public know the justice of veterans' claims and thereby contributing to the consciousness of the justice of the Legion's proposals, which has already produced results in one great legislative branch.

THE activities summarized in the foregoing paragraphs cover, of course, only a part of the Legion's work during the last eighteen months. In the space available it is possible only to mention other accomplishments, such as the distribution on Memorial Day of thousands of French Memorial Certificates to the next of kin of American soldiers who died in the war; the raising of a fund for the decoration of the graves of American soldiers abroad; the formal honors extended by posts at the reinterments of the bodies brought to the United States from overseas; the starting of a campaign for the adoption by posts of French war orphans, and the arrangements made for the distribution of Victory Medals at special ceremonies to be conducted by all posts on November 11, the anniversary of Armistice Day.

There should also be mentioned the work of the National Americanism Commission of the Legion, with its chairmen in all the Departments, and its representatives in most of the posts. This body's activities are described in detail on another page.

Nor should the importance of the Legion's function as a stabilizing in-

fluence in national sentiment be overlooked. In the last eighteen months it has been the Legion which has insisted upon official punishment of the draft dodgers and deserters when the tendency to "forget" seemed growing. The organization, by its meetings and parades, has existed as a constant reminder to the country of the necessity of keeping alive the spirit of devotion to country—and by performing this service alone it has more than demonstrated the reason for its existence.

THE actual service rendered to municipalities during public disorder or other emergencies also ranks among the organization's accomplishments. At Youngstown, Boston, Denver, Omaha, and Melrose Park, Ill., The American Legion has come forward when it seemed that public police authority was incapable of handling conditions which were menacing life and property. On all these occasions, the Legion has attempted to act purely to protect the interests of the general public, refraining from taking sides in the controversial labor questions which led up to critical labor situations.

Passing over without mention scores of other general accomplishments of the Legion, there ought not be overlooked what is perhaps the broadest measure of the success of the organization—the extent in which it has gained the confidence and respect of all the communities in which its posts have been carrying on.

The general public has become familiar with Legion aims and ideals through the work of the individual posts, and it is the firmly-established friendship of people generally toward the Legion which indicates how it has lived up to its possibilities for usefulness.

Membership in the Legion has come to have definite advantages from the public viewpoint, largely because Legionnaires have shown everywhere that they may be depended upon to give their support to all activities for the public welfare and have shown that they have no narrow, selfish interests as ex-soldiers which outweigh their broader interests as good citizens.

The Legion's Mouthpiece at Washington

National Legislative Committee Has Put In a Busy Year
Close to the Nation's Law-making Councils

NO political party in this country ever adopted a more pretentious platform than the one the last American Legion Convention put forth at Minneapolis. It covered everything from War Risk Insurance to Army nurses, and passed resolutions on practically everything and everybody in the then known ex-service world.

To have attempted to realize on a declaration of principles and policies so varied and comprehensive without a Legion megaphone down at Washington, through which the voice of the great ex-service man's organization might be made articulate, would have been to copy after those builders of Babel who sought to raise a tower to the tune of a thousand tongues.

Therefore the National Legislative Committee of The American Legion, the Legion mouthpiece at Washington. Provided for by resolution, appointed by the National Commander, and functioning as an essential cog in the Legion's national machinery, this committee during the last year has made the voice of The American Legion and the ex-service man heard in the council chambers of the nation where the law is made, in the executive offices where it is enforced, and in the hundreds and hundreds of dingy little departmental bureaus from which the actual administration is directed.

On the great question of the war's disabled and their compensation and rehabilitation; in the matter of

civil service preference for veterans; with reference to liberalizing amendments to laws governing the three great ex-service bureaus, the War Risk, the Federal Board and the Public Health Service; concerning the vastly important matter of adequate appropriations for ex-service purposes; in the fight for the Legion four-fold plan of adjusted compensation; pertaining to the matter of legislation on slackers, enemy aliens and immigration; in respect to the reorganization of the Army; on all questions and phases of questions relating to hundreds of bills covering a wide range of subjects of vital interest to ex-service men, from something as important as the Sweet Bill to something as small as the re-

The final volley. The firing squad of the Huerfano Post, Walsenburg, Col. (above), pays final honor to the body of Private John A. Furphy

Members of the Vincent B. Costello Post, Washington, D. C. (left), attending burial services in Arlington National Cemetery.— National Photo Co.

The Guard of Honor— Sentries on post (right) beside the soldier dead on Hoboken piers. — (c) Underwood and Underwood

In tribute to the dead. Funeral procession of the Huerfano Post, starting from the courthouse

At the last resting place —Pallbearers from the Huerfano Post (below) with flag-draped casket at the place of burial.

modeling and refitting of a single small hospital, and with hundreds of details looking toward an efficient and favorable administration of the many laws on the statute books dealing with ex-service men and ex-service problems—on all these affairs of high import The American Legion has spoken out through its National Legislative Committee at Washington. The result has been telling, the effect remarkable.

The task of the Legislative Committee with reference to Congress alone was stupendous. The Sixty-sixth Congress opened on December 2, 1919, and adjourned June 5, 1920. During that time there were presented for its consideration 473 bills on twenty-four different subjects directly affecting ex-service men and women. In addition to seeing that bills were drawn and introduced properly to cover all the resolutions of the Minneapolis convention of the Legion, it fell to the Legislative Committee to keep almost hourly tab on the status of every single one of these nearly five hundred bills.

Hardly a day passed but that there was an important hearing going on in one of the Committees of the House or Senate on some piece of legislation of great importance to members of the Legion and ex-service people, and at every hearing at least one of the members of the Legion committee was present to present and press the Legion standpoint.

NOT because the influence of the Committee on Congress can be completely estimated by the results obtained in appropriations for ex-service purposes, but because dollars and cents are such a striking barometer of achievement, it is not without significance that the total sum of money voted by the last session of Congress for the disabled were $358,545,000 as compared with the sum of $150,000,000 voted for the same purpose by the Sixty-fifth Congress. Not in the spirit of grab, but with a feeling of infinite concern for the welfare of the disabled, the Legion's representatives at Washington have insisted and insisted again upon appropriations of a size sufficient to take care of the Government's rehabilitation program without petty fractioning of cents or niggardly quibbling over tiny technicalities.

With reference to the program of Legion legislation as a whole, there will be remembered as some of the high spots of accomplishment the Sweet Bill, raising the monthly allowance of the disabled man in training from the pitiful pittance of $30 a month to the more comfortable, though inadequate sum of $80; the Darrow Bill, further increasing this allowance; amendments to the Civil Service law giving preference to veterans; the incorporation of the recommendations of the Legion in the new Army bill; the revision of the Articles of War and Army courts-martial; amendments to the homestead laws giving certain rights and preferences to veterans in settling on Government lands; two laws with reference to aliens, and legislation giving rank to Army nurses, authorizing the War Department to lend rifles to Legion posts and providing the privilege of retirement for emergency officers of the Navy.

Only too well will be remembered, too, the Legion's Fourfold Plan as in-

corporated in the Fordney Bill, the one great comprehensive measure for all ex-service men, and the Wason bill to buoy up the Bureau of War Risk Insurance—both outstanding pieces of legislation backed by the Legion to the limit and pressed through the lower House only to be held up in the Senate.

If the Legislative Committee could have folded its hands and rested on its oars, legislation once on the statute books, its job at Washington would have been a vastly simpler one. Legislation, however, and especially, it seems, that in the interest of ex-service men and women, has to be followed to the last ditch and then given a poke in the ribs to make it go over the top.

THE services rendered by the Washington representatives of the Legion in this respect extended over a wide field. There was, for instance, an interpretation of the law by the Surgeon General of the Army under which thousands of disabled men still in the service and in Army hospitals were to be discharged and turned loose to take their chances with the Public Health Service or any hospital they could find. The Legion, through its Legislative Committee, raised a howl sufficiently loud and long to prevent such action being taken except with the consent of the patients themselves.

There should be mentioned, likewise, the matter of preference for veterans in civil service jobs. Members of the Legion Legislative Committee have made their faces and handwriting familiar in the various Government Departments, demanding that the law on this subject should be liberally interpreted in the interest of the ex-soldier. Just as one concrete example of the results they have obtained, it may be mentioned that ninety percent of all ex-service men who have passed postal examinations got their places regardless of their standing in comparison with other candidates.

Another instance where the Legion representatives rendered a conspicuous

In its next issue

The AMERICAN LEGION Weekly

will publish

EXCLUSIVE SIGNED STATEMENTS

by

SENATOR HARDING

and

GOVERNOR COX

These statements, prepared at the request of the editors of this magazine, will discuss the issues of the coming election as seen by each major party's choice for the presidency.

service at Washington was when the recent order concerning the removal of ex-service patients in an effort to centralize them first went into effect. Although not disapproving of the policy as a whole, the Legion was quick to protest against its enforcement in individual cases where it was against the wishes and not to the interest of the ex-service men affected. Modification to suit the idea of the Legion has been promised.

Not long ago, to cite another case of service, the Comptroller of the Treasury handed down a fine-spun decision denying the Federal Board for Vocational Education the right to render such medical treatment and attention to disabled men in training as to keep them fit to pursue their courses. All efforts made by the Board and other organizations to get a reversal of this decision were in vain. The Legion Committee went in person and as a whole to see the Comptroller, and obtained not only the promise of a reconsideration but the assurance that something would be done to take care of the situation.

The list of such services could be strung out almost indefinitely, and would include not only many decisions and rulings procured from Governmental Departments favorable to ex-service men, but hundreds and hundreds of individual cases handled for members of the Legion throughout the country. The Committee has acted as a clearing house for many, many difficult tangles between Legionnaires and the Bureau of War Risk Insurance, the Vocational Board and the Public Health Service.

ON top of all this the Legislative Committee has been the connecting link between National Headquarters at Indianapolis and all bureaus and officials at Washington having anything to do with the problems and privileges of ex-service men.

The make-up of the Committee, during the greater part of the year, has been Thomas W. Miller, of Delaware, chairman; John Thomas Taylor, of Washington, D. C., general counsel; H. H. Raege, of Texas, and K. A. McRae, of Nebraska. Recently Mr. Miller resigned as chairman, and Mr. Taylor was designated to take his place.

The American Legion has by no means obtained all it asked at Washington, but its efforts for the ex-soldier have been crowned with glittering success as compared with what the veterans of the Civil and Spanish-American Wars were able to get. It did succeed in extracting from Congress, in the way of beneficial legislation and appropriations for ex-service purposes, in one year more than the Yanks of '61-'65 were able to get in thirty years, and more than the Spanish-American veterans in ten. If any political administration in this country had approached anywhere as near to writing its party platform into law as The American Legion, its stump orators would be "pointing with pride" with so much justice that it would give the opposition real cause to "view with alarm."

To summarize the actual results accomplished, even in one line sentences, makes a list almost too formidable to

A MISCELLANY OF LEGION ACTIVITIES

Reno acclaims National Commander Franklin D'Olier at a gathering of Legionnaires (above) and presents him with the key to the city

A wounded Yank (left) enjoys Legion hospitality at a lawn fete near Boston

Just kids—little guests of Claude Peltz Post (above) at a picnic at Dravosburg, Pa.

Havana's new life-savers (left): Morrie Heller, Tom Wheeldon and Harry Chemidlin of Havana Post

"And I'll see you in C-U-B-A"—Legionnaires and Senoritas (above) on the beach at Havana

A mopping-up party at parade rest: Legionnaires of Roger White Post, Fayette, Mo., snatch a minute off from the job of cleaning up the streets of their community

read, and yet there is no better reply a member of the Legion can give to the next skeptic who asks what he is going to get out of joining up, than to point him to the following brief outline of ex-service victories of a year at Washington, won largely, though of course not wholly, by The American Legion:

Law passed incorporating The American Legion.

Sweet Bill made law, raising monthly allowance of disabled soldier in training from $30 to $80, and making increase of $90,000,000 in appropriation for disabled men.

$125,000,000 voted to War Risk Insurance Bureau for death and disability claims.

$46,000,000 voted for hospitalization of ex-service men.

$550,000 voted for Mt. Alto Hospital for ex-service men.

$250,000 voted for one cent a mile furlough rates for disabled men in Army and Navy hospitals.

$295,000 voted for remodeling and refitting Army and Navy hospitals for ex-service uses.

$7,000,000 appropriated to cover increased monthly allowance for disabled men in training.

$90,000,000 voted to the Federal Board for Vocational Education.

$8,463,000 voted for twenty-six land settlement projects for ex-service men.

$21,549,000 voted for care of A. E. F. dead in keeping with policy recommended by the first Legion Convention.

Law passed authorizing transfer from War Department to Public Health Service of Army hospitals at Fort Henry, Whipple Barracks, Fort Bayard and in Cook County, Ill., providing 2,000 additional beds for disabled ex-service men.

Law passed giving disabled ex-service men receiving hospitalization from the Government privilege of buying Quartermaster supplies at cost.

Law passed providing use of National Homes for disabled volunteer soldiers for ex-service hospitalization.

Law passed authorizing War Department to lend rifles to Legion posts.

Law passed including revision of Articles of War and Army courts-martial.

Law passed increasing pay of men in Army and Navy.

Law passed giving relative rank to Army nurses.

Law passed providing the privilege of retirement for disabled officers of the Naval Emergency Corps.

Law passed authorizing War Department to lend tents to veteran organizations during encampments or conventions.

Amendments to civil service law and rulings giving certain rights and privileges to ex-service men and women.

Law passed giving ex-service men and women preferential right of sixty days to file on all public lands.

Law passed opening up to ex-service settlement 30,000 acres of land in Oregon.

Law passed authorizing Secretary of Interior to count time spent in vocational training as residence on homesteads filed by disabled men.

Law passed granting ex-service men deduction of their length of service, up to a maximum of two years, from the three years' residence necessary to establish homestead rights.

Law passed to exclude and expel from the United States aliens who are members of anarchistic and similar classes.

Law passed to deport certain undesirable aliens and to deny readmission to those convicted of conspiracy and already deported.

Circular Letter No. 345, issued by War Department, discharging large numbers of disabled men from Army hospitals before cured, modified and practically repealed.

Legion's attitude and policy represented in investigation of Federal Board for Vocational Education.

Recommendations of Legion's Committee on Military Policy written into Army Reorganization Act.

The American Legion insignia and AMERICAN LEGION WEEKLY copyrighted.

Patents obtained for American Legion emblem and Women's Auxiliary emblem.

Arrangements made with Bureau of Commercial Economics to supply to all posts of The American Legion motion picture films free of charge.

Legion's policy with reference to draft deserters and draft delinquents pressed on War Department and Department of Justice with promise of ultimate success.

10,000 acres of land, open to soldier settlement, in Oregon, saved from being turned over to a public corporation by Legion protest to Secretary of Interior.

Arrangements for the re-adoption of French War Orphans by Legion Posts handled, and perfected with Red Cross.

The Legion's Fourfold Plan of Beneficial Legislation, embodied in the Fordney Bill, engineered to victory through the House of Representatives.

The Wason Bill, amending the War Risk Insurance Act in the interest of efficiency, successfully pushed through the House of Representatives.

Complete and indexed file of the 473 bills affecting ex-service men prepared.

Complete and indexed file of all laws enacted affecting ex-service men prepared.

Thousands of claims and communications from members of the Legion and from Legion posts requiring specific assistance in various Government Departments taken care of.

Liaison maintained with Legion headquarters and service rendered in all matters having Washington end.

The Legion Committees at Work

Groups on Whose Shoulders Much of the Burden of Administration Has Rested Have Put In a Busy and Fruitful Year

ANY summary of the Legion's organization and its work in the last year would be incomplete without at least brief reference to the efforts and accomplishments of the Legion committees.

These groups of active workers, upon whose shoulders rested much of the burden of Legion administration, policy and performance, were on the job from convention to convention putting Legion words into action.

There was, to begin with, the National Executive Committee of the Legion—its legislative branch of government between conventions—composed of representatives from every Legion Department. This committee met five times during the twelve months: the day following the close of the Minneapolis convention; when it gave its approval to certain appointments of the new National Commander; the middle of December last at Washington, for a conference on War Risk Insurance, when by a long, hard week of labor many recommendations for improvement in the handling of ex-service insurance, allowances and allotments were worked out; on February 10, at Indianapolis, when a definite stand was taken for adjusted compensation, farm and home aid, land settlement and the extension of vocational training; on March 20 at Washington, when the four features indorsed at the previous Indianapolis meeting were incorporated into a scheme of legislation known as the Legion Fourfold Plan; and finally on May 18, also at Washington, when the final touches were put on the Fourfold Plan, and the whole matter laid before Congress with all the power and persuasion the Legion's representatives could exert.

Hundreds of important matters, in addition to those mentioned, came before these five sessions of the National Executive Committee. The advice and wishes of the committee also were frequently sought by the National Commander and National Headquarters by mail and telegraph on practically every question of importance concerning which there existed doubt or difference of opinion.

THE drawing of the Legion Fourfold Compensation Bill, as it was finally committed to paper and print, was the work of the Legion's Committee on Beneficial Legislation. The members of this committee, with the guidance, instruction and approval of the National Executive Committee, put the Fourfold Plan into words. When the National Executive Committee met in Washington, March 20, this work was delegated to the already existing Committee on Land Settlement and Home Aid, the members of which were A. A. Sprague of Illinois, David P. Barrows of California, J. G. Scrugham of Nevada, Galloway Harrison of Arkansas and Gilbert Bettman of Ohio. To this group were added three new members, J. G. Emery of Michigan, George F. Tyler of Pennsylvania and Judson Hannigan of Massachusetts.

The committee was set to the task of framing the Legion Fourfold Bill. The members performed their delicate and difficult job with such dispatch and efficiency that they won to their bill the almost unanimous commendation of the National Executive Committee, and after making slight changes in it at the second Washington conference in May, saw it passed by the House of Representatives.

If things have begun to run along more smoothly between the disabled ex-service man and the Federal Board for Vocational Education, the result is partially due to the activity of The American Legion Committee on Vocational Education.

Since this committee began to help the Federal Board the last week in April, more than 16,000 disabled men have been placed in training, conditions have improved several hundred percent, the morale of the men in training has gone up appreciably, an official of the Board has been placed in Legion National Headquarters for liaison purposes, and on the fifteenth of this month the Board's docket of cases, once full, overflowing and beyond control, had been absolutely cleaned up.

This remarkable accomplishment was brought about by an exhaustive study (Continued on page 29)

COMPANY CLERKS AND CHIEFS OF STAFF

Americanism Commission (right): Standing, H. H. McAnally and Robert W. Searle. Seated, David E. Finley, Jr., Arthur Woods Gerald J. Murphy (below), head of the Service Division, Indianapolis

G. H. Rennick (left), Assistant National Adjutant and Robert H. Tyndall, National Treasurer, Indianapolis

Lemuel Bolles (above), National Adjutant, Indianapolis

Russell G. Creviston (above), Director of Organization, Indianapolis On the job at Washington (left): John Thomas Taylor, of Washington, D. C., chairman of the Legion's Legislative Committee (at left) and H. H. Raege, of Texas, committee member

EDITORIAL

D Day

THE first National Convention of the Legion at Minneapolis last year opened on November 11. The Second National Convention at Cleveland will open on September 27.

The dates are historic and significant. The one is the anniversary of armed America pausing for breath on the completion of an appointed job. The second is the anniversary of a job just begun—the second day of a battle which was to last forty-five days longer, a battle in which there was to be more than a month of gruelling fighting before the full fruit of arduous endeavor could be harvested in the rupture of the Kriemhilde line.

In more homely and civilian metaphor, the one anniversary conjures up the picture of a man straightening his necktie and putting on his coat after doing up the town bully, the second the picture of a man with his coat already off, his necktie trailing over his shoulder, with the fight against the bully only fairly under way. The Legion at this date is already such a hard-hitting, tough-muscled body that it has perhaps no need to hitch its convention to a glorious date in its own infant history. But having done so, whether for sentimental reasons or for more practical considerations, it may well reflect on the coincidence.

The Legion this year meets on the anniversary of a day on which it did not stop, but went ahead. At Cleveland it must do more than consolidate its gains; it must plot out new objectives, and its record of patriotic utility in the year ahead will be measured by its ability to reach and hold them.

The Reckoning

AS The American Legion approaches the close of its fiscal year and its representatives gather for its Second National Convention, it is fit that an accounting be made of its activities and accomplishments to date, that members of the Legion may know what their membership means and counts for, that other ex-service men may have made plain to them the value of membership in the Legion, and that the public at large may come to have a better understanding of the Legion's place in the national life.

Such an accounting has THE AMERICAN LEGION WEEKLY attempted to make in this pre-convention number. Much of the space in this issue is devoted to summarizing the efforts and results of the national administration of the Legion. As impressive as such a summary may be, however, it can but chronicle the smallest fraction of the Legion's total achievement. For what has been done by the national officers and the national staff of the Legion is as nothing in comparison with the collective accomplishment of the thousands upon thousands of earnest and sincere men and women who have worked untiringly in the fifty-six state and foreign Departments of the Legion and in its 9,700 posts.

So successful has been their work that from little more than a vision when its representatives met in national assembly less than a year ago, it has become, as the representatives prepare to reconvene a second time, a great cohesive union of two million men, well organized, deeply inspired, keenly alive—a mighty association tremendously proud of its traditions of service in war and throughly awake to its possibilities of service in peace.

Prohibition of Noises

AS if the Island of Guam were not paradise enow, the governor of the island, who is also a captain in the Navy, has issued a decree forbidding whistling. The decree specifies that it is "an unnecessary and irritating noise and must be discontinued."

To some of the residents of Guam the order may seem severe. To others it cannot but be a cause for rejoicing. At any rate, the residents of Guam have no other alternative than observance. The governor has absolute authority to make laws and enforce them.

If the governor of Guam can suppress with a few taps of his typewriter such an ancient and substantial evil as whistling, what might not be accomplished in the interests of worn and debilitated nervous systems by American officials at home cloaked with like authority? The mayor of a city then, assuming his office not elective, could not only snap his fingers at the whistlers' vote but could suppress the tenor on the floor above and appropriately penalize the man next door who plays saxophone records on his phonograph at 11 P.M. He could declare an outlaw the man who runs amuck telling everybody what his grandfather did, and he could turn over to the police the chronic pessimist who constantly asserts that the world has gone to the dogs and predicts a panic next week.

Such an official, however, would probably be eventually the only law-abiding resident of his community, all his constituents being at liberty on bail bonds, conditioned on their keeping quiet.

Globe and Anchor Discipline

WHEN a few Prussians misclothed in American uniforms were held up to public condemnation after the Armistice, the scorn they received only emphasized that the late war was no field day for the martinet, the slave-driver wearing spurs, the iron-fisted autocrat accidentally given a commission with which he could not be trusted. Even with the Army's code of unquestioning obedience to every higher authority, the capricious tyrant was always in hot water—always on the defensive against retributive fair-play.

Not many hard-boiled officers were able to violate long the fundamental American conception of how one man should treat another. For the most part, the wartime Army arrived at a sensible, workable code in the relations of officers and enlisted men. The Headquarters of the Marine Corps at Washington seems to have condensed that code in a recent General Order, which reads, in part:

"The relation between officers and enlisted men should in no sense be that of superior and inferior, nor that of master and servant, but rather that of teacher and scholar. In fact, it should partake of the nature of the relation between father and son,"

Which does not mean, we conjecture, that if the scholar plays hookey he would be any less an AWOL, or if the son should stay out after-hours he would escape parental discipline. The rod would not displace K. P., nor the woodshed the brig.

THE NEW ZERO HOUR

The Honor in
From the

WE ARE PROUD, not that we devoted the eleven plants of the American Chain Company to war work for the government, but because we were able to do more than the government asked us to do, and there is no taint of profiteering on our escutcheon.

We are poorer in pocketbook because we took the government contracts.

We would have made more by meeting the regular commercial demands for Acco products.

But we are richer in honor.

Every member of the Acco family was glad to give his or her best to win the war.

We forged thousands of tons of anchor chains, chains for the steering gear, for the hoists, needed for the fighting ships and the emergency fleet.

We made chains in quantities never heard of for logging camps, for shipyards, for steel mills.

We made a million and a half or more pounds of chain for our 100,000 freight cars in France.

Seven million pounds of towing chains were needed for our motor trucks abroad, to say nothing of the chains for the artillery, for transport wagons, for the repair plants.

In addition we had to meet the demands of the railroads at home, of chains needed to harvest and move crops.

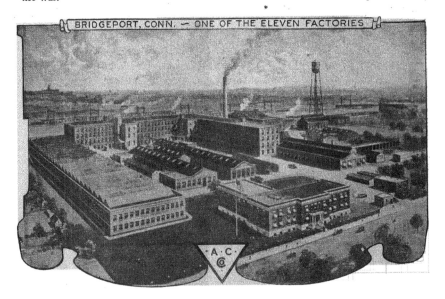

BRIDGEPORT, CONN. — ONE OF THE ELEVEN FACTORIES

Our Discharge Service.

Therefore it was impossible to meet the regular trade demands for Acco products.

For Weed Tire Chains alone among our products were we able to meet the needs of both the government and the public.

Foresight in providing a reserve supply, cooperation on the part of the public in conserving Weed Chains, and recognition on the part of the government that they are an essential in times of war, made it possible to avoid the calamity of a shortage.

Every intelligent man and woman knows that only tire chains can make motoring safe on slippery roads. Every motor car and truck owner knows that Weed

Chains are the only chains that protect and conserve tires instead of destroying them.

But Weed Chains, vital as they are to motor cars and motor trucks, represent only a small part of the activities of the Acco family, measured by tonnage or money value.

Now that we are honorably discharged from war work, we are directing the increased output of the Acco family to meet the public's demand for the Acco products, which it was impossible to supply during the war.

These Acco products are made and sold according to the same code of honor that marked our dealings with the government.

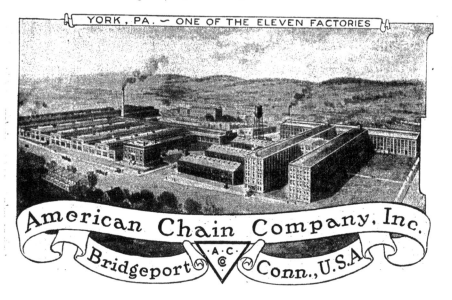

YORK, PA. — ONE OF THE ELEVEN FACTORIES

American Chain Company, Inc.
Bridgeport Conn., U.S.A.

BURSTS and DUDS

Payment is made for original material suitable for Bursts and Duds. Unavailable jokes will be returned only when accompanied by stamped, self-addressed envelope. Address Editor, Bursts and Duds, THE AMERICAN LEGION WEEKLY, 627 West 43d street, New York City.

Back to Nature

"Mandy," said the philanthropic visitor as he put a two-dollar bill in a little black hand, "your little girl looks hungry, so I'm giving her some money so that she can get a nice chicken for your dinner."

"Mandy, Jr.," said her mother as the door closed behind him. "Yo' gimme dat two dollahs. Now yo' go get dat chicken like de kind gemmun told yo', only yo' get it in de way what God meant yo' to."

Reasonable Request

"May I offer you some refreshment?" asked Boreleigh at the dance.

"Yes, thank you," replied Miss Caustique. "You might give me a few moments to myself."

The Lesser Evils

"Now, just as a matter of curiosity," began the lawyer's friend, who was seeking free advice, "what would be the best way for a man to avoid paying alimony?"

"There are two good ones," explained the legal luminary. "He can stay single or he can stay married."

Applied Anatomy

Where can a man buy a cap for his
   knee,
Or a key for a lock of his hair?
Or can his eyes be an academy,
   Because there are pupils there?
In the crown of his head what gems
   are found?
Who travels the bridge of his nose?
Does the calf of his leg become hungry
   at times
And devour the corn on his toes?
Can the crook of his elbow be sent to
   jail?
Where's the shade from the palm of
   his hand?
How does he sharpen his shoulder
   blades?
I'm hanged if I understand.

Expert at It

"Private Johnson," yelled the top kick on the returning transport as he discovered the recalcitrant lying on his bunk during the fire drill, "didn't you hear me yell, 'Everybody inside, out'?"

"Yeah," groaned Private Johnson, from the depths of gloom, "but what difference does that make to me? I've been that way since this boat started."

Hark, Hark, the Lark

Here's a letter received by an attendant in the Red Cross chapter at Lancaster, Ohio:

"Dear Miss Blank: What is this, anyway, an Army or a school for chorus girls? Here I got a letter from Washington about this here Vocal Training and I can't tell one note from another."

BUCKEYE CORNERS NEWS ITEMS

Constable Wheelright accidentally sets fire to his celluloid collar

Smart Alecks

Slick City Feller: "See that hill over there? Well, it's all bluff."

Just as Slick Farmer: "See that cow over there? Well, it's all bull."

Per Queensberry

"Do you think," asked his teacher, "it's r'ght
With your playmate in that way to fight?"
"It's the best way I know,"
   Said diminutive Joe,
"Teach me how. I'll sure make him a sight."

The Cyclone Habit

"But," declared a German prisoner at Château-Thierry, "I don't see yet how you took me a prisoner. I was one of the Storm Troops."

"Storm nothing," answered the Yank, "I come from Kansas. I'm used to it."

The Direct Hint

Colonels, like everyone else, need a bath now and then, but colonels, like everyone else, do not like to be reminded of the fact. The Y. M. C. A. had opened a swimming-pool at a certain Army camp, and as a compliment sent tickets to all the officers. After the second one arrived the colonel sat down and relieved his mind in the following letter:

"Gentlemen: Your first ticket pleased me greatly. As to your second, I'm a little surprised. If a third arrives I shall consider it an insult."

Rest Is Right

Lured by the promises of the brilliant recruiting signs in the Army's new drive, a lank Arkansas youth had let himself in for three years and was taking his first third degree from the sergeant.

"D'ya know what the command 'Rest' means?" bellowed his mentor.

"Sure," replied the rookie. "You can talk, you keep one foot in position, and you got to remain somewhere in the vicinity."

Stop, Look and Listen

In a moment of carelessness the salesman had crawled into the village taxicab. First it punctured a tire. Then it narrowly avoided a post. Then it just escaped collision with a passing buggy. Then, as a final treat, it avoided annihilation with a locomotive by a fifth of a second.

"Say," ejaculated the salesman, as he gratefully climbed out, "thank Heaven, you ain't running a merry-go-round."

"Wow! How 'bout a nip, Bill? Where'd you get it?"
"Right over there in the garage—my flivver only drinks by the quart with gas so high."

For the Safety of the Public

First New Cop: "Tis very strange. Why do the capt'n have us out here for pistol practice when he warns us that whenever we shoot off our guns in the strate we must do it in the air."

Second New Cop: "Tis to learn us to strike the target so as we can hit the air when we aim at it."

No Alternative Then

In the present recruiting campaign the Army spares no pains in displaying the attractions it offers. In Denver a man wearing the service button stood thoughtfully in front of a glaring sign which read:

"Chances for service in eight different countries. The sergeant will tell you where you can go."

"I wonder," ruminated the button-wearer dreamily, "what the seven are besides the one he used to mention so often."

Matter of Concentration

"Young man, are you thinking very seriously about marrying my daughter?"

"I wasn't, sir, but, believe me, I would before I did."

The Literary Q. M.

The new quartermaster on the good freighter *Sioux* was at the wheel and was rattled. First the ship swung madly to port, then to starboard, and then back again. The old skipper stood her antics as long as he could, and then burst forth.

"Say, son," he shouted, "I don't mind your writing your name in the old pond, but for the love of Mike, stop going back to read it."

THE VOICE of the LEGION

The Victory Medal

To the Editor: The reason why some ex-soldiers are not applying for the Victory Medal goes back to the original mistake in providing for them. There never should have been any difference in these medals, except for those of wounded men. I know dozens of old soldiers who were crazy to get in the fighting, after years of peacetime service, who were compelled to soldier in the United States while newly-drafted recruits were sent, often against their wills, direct to the fighting front. Can you blame these old heads for not wanting a medal which publishes their hard luck? Also, the basis of award is faulty. I cannot understand the ridiculous ruling which denies at least a defensive sector clasp to every man who served in Siberia. We were on the defensive there all the time against three different treacherous enemies. If the other Siberian vets feel as I do they won't accept a Victory Medal which camouflages the really hazardous service every Infantry outfit saw there. J. L. BELL
Rock Spring, Wyo.

Where to Get the Money

To the Editor: United States Senator Capper, of Kansas, declared in a speech on August 30 that one-third of the twenty-six billions spent by the Government during the war was graft, extravagance, etc. He also said:

"Recently the Supreme Court relieved the vested interests of the cruel necessity of paying income taxes on

about two billions of surplus war and peace profits. This swag is now being distributed daily as stock dividend 'war melons' and goes to swell the capital of the corporations declaring them."

About as fair a way as any to get money to compensate veterans is to extract it from the newly-made millionaires who piled up their fortunes on fat Government contracts.
Watertown Post No. 228, G. H. R.
Watertown, N. Y.

Help That Counts

To the Editor: Having read a few letters in which ex-soldiers have inquired regarding actual benefits of belonging to The American Legion, let me tell you my own experience.

After returning from the A. E. F, I found that nobody at Washington seemed to have any record of the Liberty Bonds which I had bought in 1917 out of my Army pay. After having filled out three affidavits I received no reply from Washington. After waiting a whole year, I decided to let the

Legion see what it could do. I put my case up to our State Adjutant, and, behold, last Wednesday I received three beautiful Liberty Bonds.
EDWARD C. DOZYK,
Formerly Co. B, 26th Eng.
Donora, Pa.

The Croix de Goof

To the Editor: Several weeks ago, D. Harrigan, of Glenns Ferry, Ida., said through "The Voice of The Legion" th t he still had some Gorgonzola Cheese Medalos, 2d Class, for distribution in worthy cases where the recipient had ventured far beyond the call of duty, good taste or plain crust. I want to recommend for this decoration a bird I saw in Cincinnati, O., wearing a Victory Ribbon on the front of his civilian coat.

I am gathering the facts on another man I think is worthy of nomination, a goof who pretends he almost forgot how to speak English while he was in the A. E. F. and now rings in doughboy French words while talking to his non-veteran friends on any subject and in any place. His goofiness certainly deserves a medal and when I get enough incidents to form the basis of a citation I will recommend him for the decoration.
Columbus, O. A. R. T.

Americans in France

To the Editor: So many requests are coming to the Employment Bureau of the Paris Post from young men in America who desire to come to work

Disabled service men in the carpentry class of the New England Vocational School, Rutland, Mass., build poultry brooder houses as a part of their course under the Federal Board. When they have mustered the knack of building hotels for chickens they will graduate to the building of houses

in France that we request that you give this letter publicity.

For a man to succeed in making his living in France, it is absolutely essential that he speak and write French fluently and also that he have a trade. While we have succeeded in finding employment for a great number of men, the sources will surely be exhausted very shortly. We suggest that men who desire to work in France come here only after having made a contract with an American concern with branches in France.

BEN C. HERSHFIELD
Chairman, Employment Committee
Paris Post No. 1,
Paris, France

The Garden Spot

To the Editor: In your issue of August 27, a letter from Mr. Tewson, of Toledo, O., mentions an artificial lawn in California and ordinances prohibiting the carrying of umbrellas because it never rains in California. I'd like to have the recipe for the particular brand of home brew which must have inspired his comments.

We all realize that the United States is a fine place to live in, but let me tell you that you can't get away from the fact that California is the garden spot of it.

Why is it some Easterners hate to own up to it? Is it ignorance or jealousy? If it's ignorance come out and look us over. If it's jealousy—well, we can't blame any Easterner for that. When you come, buy only a one-way ticket. It will save you the trouble of getting a refund.

CHARLES H. CUTTER
Davis, Cal.

A Regular Replies

To the Editor: In answer to C. M. R., who referred in a recent issue to the "homeless Regulars," I want to say that I well know he wasn't a Regular. The Regulars on the whole are not homeless, and furthermore, if it hadn't been for the Regulars the United States Army would have been short of officers and wouldn't have had any National Army. They are the ones who trained the new soldiers and taught them that they were not behind the counter and behind the plow. I was a Regular and will be again if there is another war. I have a brother in Siberia who has spent thirteen years

in the Regular Army and he has a home and a good one in Maysville, Ky. Therefore, it would have been better to leave the "poor, homeless Regular" out of the argument.

JESSE R. HARNEY
Ex-Sgt., Co. G, 46th Inf.
Maysville, Ky.

Who Can Tell Him?

To the Editor: I wonder if perhaps among your readers there is somebody who can explain a phenomenon that occurred, I believe, on October 10, 1918, over the battle front, looking from the highway between Jouy-en-Argonne to Nettancourt.

We were passing through a little town (I forget the name) where a lot of colored troops were unloading supplies from the train, when we noticed three thin parallel lines of clouds or smoke stretching far across the sky. They looked as if they had been made by three planes passing, throwing out smoke and cutting stunts; for the lines were far from straight. Through these lines were waves which ran perpendicular to the earth, with a drift from left to right. They looked most like waves of heat one sees rising from the earth, but they traveled with a shifting motion somewhat like the flickering of the northern lights.

Hundreds of troops were watching this display, and wondering what had caused it. Somebody suggested a mirage of the front. Others thought it might be something new by the Germans. I never heard more of it, but I have continued to wonder about it. Does anybody else remember it, and particularly, can anybody tell me what it was?

GEORGE B. VAUGHN
Hysham, Mont.

RISE AND SHINE!

To the Editor: What is all this dope we have been reading about "Improving the Infantry"? Of course all we ex-gobs read it—but it doesn't mean anything!

Wouldn't we rise and shine, though, if some gold-braider should ask for suggestions to improve the Navy? What say, gobs?

CLATE S. SPECK
Freedom Post, Pemberville, O.

To a Congressman

To the Editor: The following lines are dedicated to a Congressman who opposed veterans' compensation:

Before we ventured over there
You smote your knee, you tore your hair;
You swore by your granduncle's beard
That every lad who volunteered
To do his meek and humble share
To drive the Teuton from his lair
Would earn undying gratitude;
With honeyed phrase and platitude,
You lauded us unto the sky
As saviors of humanity.

But now that all the world is safe,
With nothing left for us to strafe,
We find, alas! that you are prone
To use the calm, judicial tone.
You say to us that duty's sense
Should be sufficient recompense;
You hoped you'd never see the day
That patriots would ask for pay;
Why, we've a monumental gall
To ask for anything at all!

MORAL
A man may pat us on the back
And spout the old familiar clack,
And smite his knee and tear his hair,
And twist his digits in the air.
But words of gold soon turn to dross—
We get for ours the double-cross.

WILLIAM LOSSONE
Melrose, Mass.

Why a "Doctor"?

To the Editor: In your issue of August 27, under the caption, "Pro-Insignia," appears a letter signed by F. D. Pilkham, Boston, Mass., in which he discusses the question of whether former officers should wear their insignia of former rank in American Legion parades or on other occasions.

He takes exceptions to the remarks of one signing himself "Comrade" in your issue of July 30, in which "Comrade" deprecates the wearing of insignia by a former officer. I quite agree with Mr. Pilkham's views, but I take exception to this sentence, viz., "If our friend (I suspect he is a doctor) takes off his oak leaves and nothing more, what does he look like?"

I want to ask, why a doctor?

I wish Mr. Pilkham had been present at a dressing station near Nantillois, France, October 1, 1918, where the writer, who is a doctor, had two of his doctors killed by one shell and two others wounded, while two D. S. C.'s were won by doctors for bravery under fire.

ROBERT B. SHACKELFORD, M. D.
Warrenton, Va.

Anybody Remember It?

To the Editor: While in the Hospital Horace at Epinal, the only American soldier there, I was often given a treat musically by four English soldiers of the Middlesex Regiment. I have tried often to recall one of their favorite songs, but can remember only these words of it:

Pity the poor civilian sitting beside his fire—
Who wouldn't be a soldier—
Oh, oh, oh, it's a lovely war.
What do you want with eggs and 'am
When you've got plum and apple jam?
For us right turn, and what do you do with
the money you earn?
For, oh, oh, oh it's a lovely war.

It's a snappy tune and I should be much pleased if any of your readers could give you the whole of it for publication.

HARRY P. DAVIS
Ex-5th Division
Houston, Tex.
1127 Jackson Boulevard

THE LEGION COMMITTEES AT WORK

(Continued from page 20)

and analysis of the whole vocational rehabilitation situation. Gerald J. Murphy, head of the Legion's Service Department, Lemuel Bolles, National Adjutant, and Marquis James of The American Legion News Service, were the members of the committee. Mention, too, should be made of the representative of the Federal Board, Walter F. Shaw, assistant to the head of the Board, who worked with the committee and who did much to make the committee's program of cooperation between the Legion and the Board a success.

NO committee of the Legion has had a harder job and none has acted with more determination and purpose than the Legion Committee on Hospitalization. This committee, of which Abel Davis of Illinois is chairman, and which includes Dr. T. Victor Keene of Indiana, Mrs. Wendell Phillips of New York, Dr. Harry E. Mock of Illinois, H. H. Raege of Washington, D. C., and A. A. Sprague of Illinois, was not authorized until the May meeting of the National Executive Committee, and of course did not get down to work until some time thereafter.

It was at the instance of this committee that the conference was held of representatives from the Bureau of War Risk Insurance, the Vocational Board, the Public Health Service, the Medical Departments of the Army and Navy and the National Home for Disabled Volunteer Soldiers, which resulted in the establishment of much closer liaison between all these government agencies in the handling of hospitalization for ex-service men.

Members of this committee, too, acting with and through the National Legislative Committee, used their influence in persuading Congress to make the appropriation of $46,000,000 for hospitalization to one man, the Director of the Bureau of War Risk In-

surance, and to make him responsible for its use. They have also, with much help from National Headquarters and Legion State officials, made a thorough investigation of conditions in nearly all of the 1,000 hospitals in which ex-service men are being treated.

THE resolutions of the last National Convention with reference to the reorganization of the Army and a permanent military policy for the nation have been pressed upon Congress by the Legion Committee on Military Policy, with the result that in the new Army Reorganization Act there are to be found many of the features indorsed by The American Legion.

This committee, as it was at first composed, consisted of Allan A. Tukey, of Nebraska, first vice-commander of the Legion, chairman; F. W. Galbraith of Ohio, Milton J. Foreman of Illinois, Henry L. Stimson of New York, Thomas W. Miller of Delaware, and R. W. Llewellen of Washington. The committee appeared twice before the Senate Committee on Military Affairs in December, 1919, and was represented by Mr. Miller before the House Committee on January 16.

Representatives of all the Departments were called together in an informal conference at Indianapolis in February 9, and the status of military legislation in Congress thoroughly gone into. Following this the committee was reorganized to include H. L. Opie of Virginia, L. R. Gignilliat of Indiana, William J. Donovan of New York, Horace C. Stebbins of New York, Benson W. Hough of Ohio, Frank A. Warner of Nebraska, Ransom H. Gillette of New York, and E. L. Logan of Massachusetts. This committee appeared before the Senate Committee on Military Affairs on March 1, and explained the views of the Legion Army Reorganization Act as then framed.

THE publication of THE AMERICAN LEGION WEEKLY has been the job of the Legion Publication Committee. The annual report to the national convention of this committee will show that the official organ of the Legion, despite serious labor troubles, transportation difficulties and other handicaps affecting the entire publishing industry during the first few months of the magazine's existence, has already come to be generally recognized as an important national publication. It also will show that the magazine has not only been self-supporting ever since, because of enormously increased costs of production, it went into fatigue garb, but has been returning a profit upon each issue published. The fact that more than $250,000 worth of future advertising space has already been contracted for is indicative of the confidence which advertisers are placing in the magazine.

The members of the Publication Committee are George d'Utassy, New York, Chairman; National Commander Franklin D'Olier; National Adjutant Lemuel Bolles; National Treasurer Robert H. Tyndall; DeLancey Kountze, of New York; Frederick B. Wells, of Minneapolis; David M. Goodrich, of New York; Matthew H. Murphy, of Birmingham, Ala.; G. Edward Buxton, Jr., of Providence; Frank Knox, of Manchester, N. H.; G. Henry Hathaway, of New York; F. W. Galbraith, Jr., of Cincinnati; Benjamin Dibble, of San Francisco, and Milton J. Foreman, of Chicago.

The members of the Publication Committee comprise the membership of the Board of Directors of the Legion Publishing Corporation. Mr. D'Olier, as National Commander is ex-officio president of the corporation, Mr. Buxton is vice-president, Mr. Bolles is secretary and Mr. Tyndall is treasurer.

The Americanism Commission and Its Task
Originally Acting as a Clearing House for Policies, It has Grown and Rendered Constructive Service Throughout the Country

THE National Americanism Commission of the Legion, which was formed at the last convention, "to foster and perpetuate a one hundred percent Americanism" in accordance with the terms of the preamble to the Constitution, closes its first year of service with a smoothly-functioning organization at work.

With headquarters in full operation in New York City, Americanism chairmen at the helm in each State, field representatives who have toured every department on the job, and Americanism committees actively serving in many posts, the enterprise of forming a nation-wide Americanism organization within the Legion is well on its way to completion.

A survey of the activities of the Commission shows that much work already has been accomplished, and a number of beneficial movements that,

promise success have been launched. One of the most recently undertaken campaigns is that for the welfare of the 17,000 disabled veterans still in hospitals. Posts in hospital towns have been called upon in the move for the wounded men, and have been directed to provide them with visitors and with advice and aid on their discharge from the institutions.

A second nation-wide project calls for obtaining the names and destinations of all immigrants at the Port of New York. This information is to be forwarded to the Americanism chairmen of the States to which the immigrants are going. Posts in the localities where the immigrants intend to settle are to be informed of their coming, and arrangements made for members of the local Americanism Committee and of the Women's Auxiliary to call upon them and extend practical

help, such as showing the newcomers where they can learn English, how to take out their first papers, and so forth.

ORIGINALLY the National Americanism Commission acted as a clearing house for policies, and information and bulletins suggesting activities were issued to Departments and posts. Eventually the bulletins were collected into a pamphlet, 10,000 copies of which were distributed. This pamphlet dealt with such subjects as the formation and aims of the Commission; organization of Americanism work by posts; getting the support of the community for Americanism; co-operation with Community Service, the Red Cross and other organizations; education of aliens; better schools and better paid teachers; parent associations; public school athletics; formation of a speakers' bureau; citizenship ceremonies and celebration of national holidays; the policeman as a factor in Americanism; assistance to the Boy Scouts, and the advantages of the public library.

The activities set on foot by the Commission are varied. Legion members in Washington, Oregon, Montana and Idaho were appointed on a committee to fight the dissemination of disloyal propaganda in the Northwest. A plan was worked out to help ex-service men in the State prisons of New York to start life anew on their release through putting them in touch with the Legion. A partial list of the activities of the Commission in the various States includes: Securing the passage of laws requiring the teaching of Americanism in schools; supplying speakers for schools on patriotic and other occasions; agitating the extension of rural educational facilities; helping ex-service men to become naturalized, and engineering local "clean-up" campaigns.

THE work of the Commission naturally has differed in separate States according to existing conditions. In some States the problem of Americanizing the foreign-born has been the paramount issue, and in others the educational problem has been foremost.

Arthur Woods, chairman of the National Americanism Commission, is directing its activities from the New York headquarters, with David E. Finley, Jr., secretary, as his right-hand man. Also working from New York are the field representatives, Robert W. Searle, P. Churchill Goettel, Lowell R. Dulon and Clifford N. Baker.

Other members of the Commission besides Mr. Woods and Mr. Finley are J. Ward Arney, Idaho; Edgar W. Baird, Pennsylvania; Philip R. Bangs, North Dakota; Hiram Bingham, Connecticut; Edson K. Bixby, Oklahoma; Edward A. Fitzpatrick, Wisconsin; August H. Gansser, Michigan; Peyton H. Hoge, Jr., Kentucky; Charles F. H. Johnson, New Jersey; Frank Knox, New Hampshire; Rogers McVeagh, Oregon; John MacVicar, Iowa; Fraser Metzger, Vermont; Frank L. Sieh, South Dakota.

THE LEGION LIBRARY

Through the medium of THE AMERICAN LEGION WEEKLY, The American Legion expects to assemble a complete library covering the field of American activity in the great war. It is intended ultimately to assemble this library in a room of its own, preferably at National Headquarters. Books received in the office of this magazine for inclusion in the library are listed on receipt, and thereafter in most cases noticed in reviews.

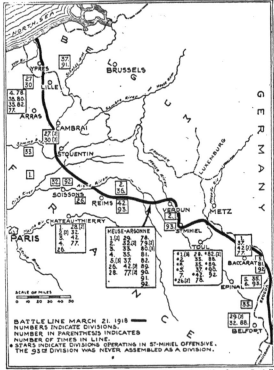

BATTLE LINE MARCH 21, 1918 ━━━
NUMBERS INDICATE DIVISIONS.
NUMBER IN PARENTHESIS INDICATES NUMBER OF TIMES IN LINE.
• STARS INDICATE DIVISIONS OPERATING IN ST-MIHIEL OFFENSIVE.
THE 93ᴿᴰ DIVISION WAS NEVER ASSEMBLED AS A DIVISION.

The A. E. F.'s fighting record on the Western Front.—From "Our Greatest Battle," by Frederick Palmer (Dodd, Mead & Co.)

Books Received

FORGING THE SWORD. *The Story of Camp Devens.* By William J. Robinson. The Rumford Press, Concord, N. H.

YANK—THE CRUSADER. By Earl C. Van Zandt. Walter C. Erickson, 1336 York Street, Denver, Colorado.

BOOKS IN THE WAR. *The Romance of the Library War Service.* By Theodore Wesley Koch. Houghton Mifflin Company, Boston and New York.

WITH THE Y. M. C. A. IN FRANCE. By Harold C. Warren. Fleming H. Revell Company, New York and Chicago.

FIRST REFLECTIONS ON THE CAMPAIGN OF 1918. By R. M. Johnston. Henry Holt and Company, New York.

AMERICAN GUIDE BOOK TO FRANCE AND ITS BATTLEFIELDS. By E. B. Gary, O. O. Ellis and R. V. D. Magoffin. The Macmillan Company, New York.

NINTH COMPANY, TWENTIETH ENGINEERS FORESTRY. *Its Story by Its Men.* Printed by Lodi Printing & Rubber Stamp Co., Lodi, California.

RANGING IN FRANCE WITH FLASH AND SOUND. By Sergeant Jesse R. Hinman. *History of the Second Battalion, 29th Engineers in France During the World War.* Press of Dunham Printing Company, Portland, Oregon.

THE STORY OF THE FIRST GAS REGIMENT. By James Thayer Addison. Houghton Mifflin Company, Boston and New York.

THE WAR ROMANCE OF THE SALVATION ARMY. By Evangeline Booth and Grace Livingston Hill. J. B. Lippincott Company, Philadelphia.

OFFICIAL HISTORY OF 82ND DIVISION, A. E. F. Written by Divisional Officers designated by the Division Commander. The Bobbs-Merrill Company, Indianapolis.

AMERICAN ENGINEERS BEHIND THE BATTLE LINES IN FRANCE. By Robert K. Tomlin, Jr. McGraw-Hill Book Company, Inc., 239 West 39th Street, New York.

TWELFTH U. S. INFANTRY. *Its Story by Its Men.* The Knickerbocker Press, New York.

A HISTORY OF THE 305TH INFANTRY. By Frank B. Tiebout, Capt. 305th Infantry, U. S. A. Published by the 305th Infantry Auxiliary, 189 Madison Avenue, New York.

AA Credit

"SOMETIMES paydays were far apart." That sentence might stand in any A. E. F. outfit history (except that a motion to eliminate the word "sometimes" could be in order in most cases), but in this instance it happens to have been written by Chaplain Evan Alexander Edwards in "From Doniphan to Verdun," the official history of the 140th Infantry, Thirty-Fifth Division. "Sometimes," as the chaplain rightly has it, "paydays were far apart—or the men were not lucky—and the soldiers asked for credit. Thousands of francs stood in the regiment at times 'jaw-bone,' expressive slang. There were times when $2,000 was owed by the men. It is a splendid tribute to the honesty of the 140th that $15 will cover the unpaid bills of the men who came home."

All About Brest

CHARLES M. TOBIN was a major in the Twenty-seventh Division who, after the Armistice, was sent to Brest and made, among other things, historian of Base Section No. 5. "I received permission from the commanding general," he writes, "to write the history of Base Section No. 5. Finding the public fed up on war books, however, I could make no better arrangement with a publishing house than the promise that they would put out the book if I could get a thousand subscribers. To date I have had two hundred replies.

"The thought occurred to me," he says, "that you might be willing to help me get the knowledge of this fact before the Legion, for I am sure that many of the men who were at Brest will be glad to have a history of the war where they took an important part. I am seeking no profit from this book; my one idea is to get it in print, that something may be said for those men who served in the line of communications, and to whom little glory came in any form." Mr. Tobin's address is 561 Spreckels Building, San Diego, Cal.

So far as the Legion Librarian is concerned, Brest is a better place to read about than to be at, particularly with the war going on.

Where the War Was Won

A GOOD guide book is something more than a street directory and hotel catalogue of the region it describes. If it is written rightly, it should make interesting reading for the man who has to do his traveling in his arm-chair—a method that is not altogether satisfactory, but which has its compensations in the speed with which the sedentary voyager can cover the ground, the minimized expense, his freedom from every social convention (including dress) and the utter impossibility of tipping.

Of such a sort are the Michelin Illustrated Guides to the Battlefields, published, with a legitimate eye to business, by the manufacturers of the tire of that name, and "dedicated to the memory of our employes who died gloriously for their country." Of the ten volumes in this series which have been published to date, the three dealing with the part played by America in the war will naturally be of chief interest to former members of the A. E. F. These three deal with the second battle of the Marne, the battle of St. Mihiel, and the battle of the Meuse-Argonne.

The purpose of a guide book is to tell where to go, how to get there, and what to see, and this the Michelin Guides do without waste of space and with many visual helps. Photographs and maps are used not so much to illustrate the text as to amplify and clarify it. The Michelin Guides are by far the most satisfactory battlefield handbooks that have yet been published.

CARRYING ON

Post correspondents: What is your Post doing? Tell it here. Copy for this department supplied by The American Legion News Service, 627 West 43d Street, New York City

THE last two months have been convention season in The American Legion. During this time most of the Departments have held their meetings, transacted their business, elected officers, chosen delegates to the National Convention and given these delegates the instructions which will guide their actions at Cleveland.

In each of the forty-eight States has one of these conventions taken place, and in several places outside the territorial United States. Those Departments which have not held their meetings within the last eight or nine weeks did so earlier in the year.

A high note of enthusiasm was the predominant characteristic of all these meetings. Without exception they were as successful as have been all big Legion gatherings. They exhibited a wideawake interest in affairs affecting the ex-service man and affairs affecting his country. They threshed out and decided problems affecting their Department organization, administration and activity and cast their votes upon matters of activity and policy which will be decided by the National Convention.

It is upon the resolutions passed by these State conventions that the work of the National Convention will be based. The recommendations made by each Department will be considered by the representatives of all the other Departments, and if they meet with the approval of the majority will become the policy of the Legion as a whole.

The problems decided by the various conventions differed widely in various sections, but several subjects, such as assistance to the war disabled and beneficial legislation for the ex-service man, were universally considered. A tabulation of the thousands of resolutions passed which affect national policy is now being prepared at National Headquarters for the consideration of the National Convention.

The lessons learned from the practical experience of the past year were unquestionably of great value in enabling the delegates to the conventions to make decisions and formulate new plans, and the value of these conventions in promoting efficiency and cooperation is already becoming apparent.

Although much business was transacted at all the conventions, the delegates found time for amusement. Many excursions, picnics, entertainments and reunions were staged. Local Legion posts invariably acted as official hosts at the State meetings and veterans of other wars frequently were entertained as guests of honor.

AS part of its plan for a great Victory Medal celebration, the Harold H. Bair Post, of Hanover, Pa., hopes to have Armistice Day made a holiday. The Post intends to get medals for all veterans in the vicinity regardless of whether or not they are Legionnaires, and to provide them for the relatives of deceased service men. So

Photo by A. H. Blackinton

"I'll say it's chow!" Four hundred disabled buddies from the hospitals in and around Boston were guests at a horse show given for them under the auspices of The American Legion of Massachusetts on the estate of Louis K. Liggett, Chestnut Hill. Automobiles were provided to bear the wounded soldiers and sailors to the scene

successful was the Post's latest minstrel show that it has been decided to give one annually. This affair netted the Post $2,700, and a block dance brought in $500. A drive will be started early this autumn for funds with which to purchase or build a home for the Legion.

The *Argonne Post Weekly*, published by the Argonne Post, of Des Moines, Iowa, has joined the rapidly mounting list of new Legion publications. Its policy is to promote the interests of Argonne Post, ex-service men, the Legion, and all patriotic organizations in the vicinity. Frank F. Miles is editor.

Through the distribution of pamphlets and posters the J. W. Person Post, of Brooklyn, N. Y., expects to boom its drive for new members. The Post bowling team is challenging the best teams in New York and Brooklyn.

CHOW! "Soupee, soupee, soupée without a single bean, porkee, porkee, porkee without a bit of lean." It was Army stuf all right at the banquet the Richard L. Briscoe Post, of Pecos, Tex. Cast your eyes over this menu:

Celery a la Seldom
Baby Shrapnel Cal. 45   Redhot Bullets
Young Weepers
Ox Tongue a la Camouflage
Army and Navy Christmas Dinner, Special
Au Marine Spuds
Bayonet Points
Red Cross Salad with Salvation Army Sauce
Week End Pass Dessert
American Punch
(That beat the Hun)
Cigars   Cigarettes

Legionnaires of the Richland Post, Olney, Ill., did "squads east" in an ex-

hibition drill at an indoor Chautauqua held for the benefit of the Post. The affair was such a success that the town intends to hold it every year.

A sham battle, depicting scenes from the Champagne-Marne defensive, was put on by the Floyd Minch Post, of Worland, Wyo., at the county fair. Legionnaires showed the work of the doughboys, and artillery fire was portrayed by fireworks. In addition to staging the sham battle the Post took over and operated all the concessions at the fair. The formation of a Woman's Auxiliary is adding to the activities of the Post.

It is safe to assert that there was talk of C. C.'s and iodine when the Reese Davis Post, of Scranton, Pa., entertained the Lackawanna County Medical Society at Lily Lake Farm, Dalton, Pa. The Post was organized in July, 1919, to keep together the medical, dental and veterinarian veterans of the county. The re-adoption of several French orphans is planned.

"COMRADES of the Legion," the latest march of John Philip Sousa, composer, has been dedicated to The American Legion. During the war Mr. Sousa served as a lieutenant commander in the Naval Reserve.

Published reports that a post in Bronx County, N. Y., intended to "picket" meetings of Socialist candidates were pronounced unfounded after investigation by New York Department headquarters. "The American Legion," said Hugh W. Robertson, assistant to the Department commander, "does not intend to impair its greatest asset, namely, goodwill and public confidence, through any reckless or overt acts."

A membership record "thirty percent better than perfect" is the modest claim of T. P. Johnston Post of Mt. Gilead, O. Preceding the nation-wide membership push, officers of the Post made a cursory investigation and decided there were approximately one hundred ex-service men and women in the community. But in "going out and getting 'em" the membership committee discovered one hundred and thirty eligibles and enrolled every one in the Legion.

The former home of the G. A. R. Post in New Paris, O., has been turned over to the Clarence Teaford Post of The American Legion as a permanent clubhouse.

MANY interesting features are on the program of the carnival arranged by the Windsor Terrace Post, of Brooklyn, N. Y., which opens tomorrow at Park Circle, that city, to run until October 2. In a girls' popularity contest, the winner will be crowned Queen of the Carnival, and will receive a diamond ring. Two other rings also will be given for second and third places in the contest. In order to assist the Americanism program of the Legion, the Post will award a prize to the child submitting the best essay on Americanism. The proceeds of the carnival will go to the Post's building fund.

To crystallize the sentiment of its members on various controversial issues, the Moultrie County Post, of Sullivan, Ill., held an extensive discussion and then adopted resolutions designed to serve as instructions for the Post's delegates to state and national conventions. The resolutions favor the Legion's four-fold optional compensation plan and recommend that the right be given the State and National Legion organizations "to use their power judiciously in non-partisan support of political candidates who are both capable and friendly toward the great principles for which The American Legion stands."

Several posts in the Department of Massachusetts, wrote State Headquarters as to the advisability of paying out of their own treasuries an amount sufficient to cover the per capita tax for their entire enrolled membership, in order to present their maximum strength at the recent Department convention. While not entirely approving of the idea, Department officials interposed no objection, in view of the fact that the different posts taking this action expressed their confidence in being able to gather in the dues of delinquent members prior to the National Convention, and the payments were made to avoid possible delays that might reduce the post's representation.

At their recent convention, Legionnaires of the Department of Panama voted to interrogate the Governor of the Panama Canal regarding the promotion policy with respect to Canal employes who were furloughed to the military or naval service during the war. If the Governor makes a ruling unfavorable to ex-service men, the Secretary of War will be appealed to for relief, according to the convention's decision.

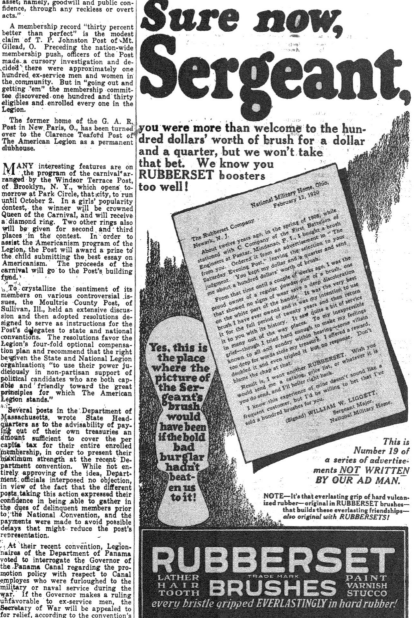

The Big Sister of the Legion

She Knitted Our Socks and Sweaters When We Were at War— Now She's the Women's Auxiliary

VERILY, the old order changeth! That phrase, far from being enlisted to introduce an unexpurgated discourse on "The Future of America and Other Problems," is merely a commonplace expression hooked up with the distinctly modern trend of development in The American Legion. For a review of one phase of its growth during the last year discloses that what many undoubtedly at first regarded as The American Legion is not alone The American Legion.

The same thing applies to the nation. The word "voters" formerly meant some thirty millions of men, more or less. After the smoke cleared from Tennessee's legislative battlefield, it meant those men and some twenty-seven million women, too.

Similarly, what was, in name and in fact, The American Legion a year ago, today is that Legion plus more than fifty thousand women compactly united within it, and constituting its Women's Auxiliary. Distinctly, in the public mind, the Legion has been pictured as a man's organization. The record of

[c] Harris & Ewing

MISS JULIA C. STIMSON, *superintendent of the Army Nurse Corps, overseas veteran of twenty-four months' service, and an active member of Jane A. Delano Post of The American Legion, Washington, D. C., is the first representative of her sex to take her place as an officer in the military organization of the United States. The Secretary of War recently gave her a commission as major under the provisions of the army reorganization bill granting rank to army nurses. Major Stimson was chief nurse of the American Red Cross for the seven months prior to the Armistice, when she was made Director of the Nursing Service of the A. E. F. Upon her return to the United States in June, 1919, she was made first acting superintendent and later superintendent of the Army Nurse Corps.*

[c] Brown Bros.

Mrs. George Alexander Wheelock, commander of Barbara Frietchie Post, Manhattan, who was elected county treasurer by the New York County Executive Committee

the year just passed reveals that a considerable portion of the Legion structure rests on women's shoulders.

Through circumstances beyond its own and everyone else's control, the Legion auxiliary was figuratively born wearing hobble skirts. She made a valiant effort, but inevitably lagged behind Big Brother, who reeled off membership miles at the rate of 25,000 a week.

But considered in any other light except that of comparison with the masculine Legion element, the Auxiliary's record of growth during the year has been stupendous. Now, toward the end

of Massachusetts and Minnesota are in a neck-and-neck race for first place among the States, having the largest number of regularly chartered units, Massachusetts, with 104, having a shade the edge on Minnesota, which, after having held the lead for several months, recently was passed by the New England commonwealth. At this writing, there are 100 chartered auxiliary units in the Department of Minnesota, 85 in Illinois, 69 in New York and 68 in Michigan and the same number in Pennsylvania.

PRIOR to the first Legion convention at Minneapolis, several women's organizations made proposals to the temporary executive committee for affiliation as the official women's organization of the Legion. But the convention decided none was sufficiently representative of the relatives of ex-service men of the World War, and drafted an eligibility clause for the formation of the Legion's own affiliated body. The present National Executive Committee has provided for the holding of State organization meetings in each State as soon as one auxiliary unit has been formed for every two posts.

Both within Departments and posts, the establishment of auxiliary units has been handicapped through inability to give this work the attention it deserved by reason of the vast amount of detailed effort attending the vast growth and development of the older branch of the organization, and so far no State has chartered a sufficient number of units to permit of the holding of a departmental auxiliary caucus under the committee's ruling.

Official recommendations on the subject of the auxiliary caucus, however,

of September, there are approximately 1,300 chartered units attached to Legion posts in all parts of the world, including one in Alaska, one in Paris, two in Hawaii and one each in Panama and Cuba.

THESE units have a combined total enrollment of 50,000 wives, mothers, sisters and daughters of ex-service men, and their organization has come in recent months to be, affectionately referred to as "The Big Sister of the Legion." What the auxiliary units have done, especially in a social and economic way, to contribute to the success of Legion activities and the civic betterment enterprises of the Posts to which they are attached, is indelibly written on the minds and hearts of the hundreds of Legion posts enjoying their organized assistance.

As this is written, the Departments

Mrs. Frank Moore, president Women's Auxiliary, Thomas Dismuke Post, Houston, Texas

based upon experiences of the year just ending, will be made to the Cleveland convention, and it is believed that plans soon will be executed to make the auxiliary, in membership as in every other way, the really big "Big Sister of the Legion" by the time the next convention rolls around.

SOME of the members of the Women's Auxiliary, it would seem, are born and not made. From W. R. Knapp Post, of St. Johnsbury, Vt., comes word that its auxiliary has taken in the youngest member of all, five-weeks-old Miss Patricia Mary Tierney. Two young ladies, aged ten and eleven months respectively, were enrolled recently by the auxiliary of the Gothenburg, Neb., Post, while the auxiliary of Austin E. Hanscom Post, of Willman, Minn., signed up a member eleven months old.

What the women's organization stands for is well expressed by one of its members, Mrs. Figg-Hoblyn, who at the installation of officers of the auxiliary at a meeting of the Santa Barbara, Calif., Post thus outlined its aims:

"The exact meaning of the word, auxiliary, is, I believe, 'helper.' Whatever you plan to do, we stand here ready to help, ready to respond to your call.

"In the preamble to your Constitution, which is also ours, among other things, you say, 'We associate ourselves together to make right the master of might, to promote peace and good will on earth, to safeguard and transmit to posterity the principles of justice, freedom and democracy; to consecrate and sanctify our comradeship by our devotion to mutual helpfulness.'

"These are stirring words that strike an answering chord in the hearts of women; for who better than they know how important it is that right and not might should rule the world?

"'To safeguard the principles of justice and freedom.' To fight for these principles, some went overseas, others drilled in the dreary camps at home, and others were called to make the supreme sacrifice—to give their lives for the cause.

"Remember that the auxiliary, though not yet formed, was with you then. Your mothers, wives and sisters were behind you, and suffered when you did. It was not given to them to do anything spectacular. They just knitted socks and sweaters to keep you warm; just wrote you letters to keep you cheerful—even when their hearts were breaking; just did whatever came to hand and kept the home fires burning.

"Now you are back—a conquering army, and we are proud of you—proud of our men, proud to be an auxiliary to a Legion who wrought so nobly for justice and for freedom.

"In the face of what you have done, what we can do seems very small, but life is composed of little things, and from tiny seeds big trees may grow. In the future we plan to do many things, some large and some small.

"To visit those that are sick and aid them in every way; to take part in public questions of importance that may come up.

"As you fought in the past for what was right and we were allowed the privilege of ministering to you, so today when problems come up to be solved and issues to be fought, we, the auxiliary, are here not to do your work for you, but to do the little that we can to uphold your hands."

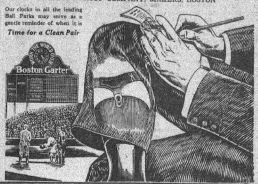

'TELLING THE WORLD ABOUT THE LEGION

How The American Legion News Service Is Keeping the Organization Daily before the Public

BILL BROWN, late of A. P. O. 764 and now of Kewanee, Ill., picks up a copy of his evening paper before supper and runs his eye up and down its columns. Pretty soon they light on an item that interests Bill. It tells how The American Legion is planning to distribute the Victory Medals on Armistice Day with celebrations in thousands of posts. Bill isn't a member of the Legion but he'd like to get in on the celebration and he's entitled to do so. He drops around to the local post to put in his application for the medal and comes out of the office a Legionnaire.

A. B. Smith, of New York City, average American citizen of middle age, buys his morning paper on the way to business. In it there is the story of a Legion post that brought order out of chaos in a little Texas oil-boom town. Mr. Smith hitherto had the vaguest idea of what the Legion stood for. Now he understands.

Joe Jones, on his farm in Kansas, lifts his favorite weekly out of the mail box by the gate and sits down on the front porch to see what's up in the world. He finds two columns of news about The American Legion and a picture or so. This is pie for Joe, who belongs to the post in the next town. He spends an interested half hour reading about what other posts are doing and comes across some War Risk Insurance information that is very important to him because he hadn't been able to get to the last two meetings of his post.

And so it goes. Bill Brown, of Kewanee, who joined the Legion; Smith of New York, who found out what the Legion stands for, and Joe Jones, Kansas Legionnaire, whose insurance problem was solved, each represents thousands of persons who are being reached every day in the countrywide publicity sent out by The American Legion News Service.

NEWS of The American Legion now is appearing regularly in more than 4,000 morning, evening and weekly papers because the News Service puts it there. And it is being printed by editors because it is real news about real men. The News Service, in the two months of its existence, has developed into a great agency for placing the activities of the Legion before millions of newspaper readers. Also, it provides THE AMERICAN LEGION WEEKLY with Legion news and features.

The headquarters of the News Service are located at 627 West Forty-third Street, New York. Branch bureaus are in Indianapolis and Washington. To headquarters correspondents appointed in every post of the Legion send the news and gossip of their activities, and from this mountain of "copy" the material is culled for releases to be sent over the country.

Some of these stories are sent out

over the great wire services of the Associated Press, the United Press Association and the International News Service. Others go out through the Newspaper Enterprise Association and other news and picture-distributing syndicates. Still others are mailed direct to the editors of newspapers in every State and in almost every town that boasts a newspaper. Legion publications also are supplied with news by this service. A special Legion department, two columns long, is provided each week to the smaller newspapers by arrangement with the Western Newspaper Union, which serves 1,000 of these influential local journals.

IT is the aim of The American Legion News Service to reach a newspaper in every town in which there is a post of the Legion in order to provide the people of that town and the Legionnaires with news of the activities of the organization. The direct service is provided without charge to 2,500 newspapers. If you would like to see your home town paper printing this news of the Legion it is simply a matter of asking the editor to apply for "copy" from The American Legion News Service.

To the Legionnaires acting as post correspondents the thanks of the News Service are due. Besides the local publicity they obtain their posts, theirs are the stories, photographs and ideas which go out to the great and the small newspapers of the country from New York headquarters. Out of the mass of stories submitted only a few each week, of course, are selected for instant telegraph and mail distribution, but those few are read by millions. Others go in the weekly news letter, and still others are released once every three weeks in a special page of "plate." Every line that comes into the office is read with a view to publication in THE AMERICAN LEGION WEEKLY.

The efficiency of the News Service depends, of course, upon the support and cooperation it receives from the posts. If your post has not yet appointed a correspondent it is missing an opportunity to help the rest of the Legion and it is overlooking an opportunity to get publicity and attention.

A story for the News Service may come from a post of twenty men in the Arizona desert just as easily as from one of a thousand in New York or San Francisco, and once put out on the Legion News Service it travels from coast to coast. It may come from a man who never had written a line for publication or it may come from a trained reporter. You do not have to be a post correspondent to send in news. Every Legionnaire as likely as not has bottled up in him a crackerjack yarn that the News Service would jump at. If you think you've got one, shoot it along—the News Service will do the rest.

The director of the News Service is Marquis James, of Oklahoma, formerly editor of THE AMERICAN LEGION WEEKLY and later national director of publicity. On the New York staff are James E. Darst, of Missouri, and Steuart M. Emery, of New Jersey. Herbert H. Updegraff, of California, is in charge of the Indianapolis Bureau. The Washington correspondent is J. W. Rixey Smith, of Virginia.

'TELLING THE WORLD ABOUT THE LEGION

How The American Legion News Service Is Keeping the Organization Daily before the Public

BILL BROWN, late of A. P. O. 764 and now of Kewanee, Ill., picks up a copy of his evening paper before supper and runs his eye up and down its columns. Pretty soon they light on an item that interests Bill. It tells how The American Legion is planning to distribute the Victory Medals on Armistice Day with celebrations in thousands of posts. Bill isn't a member of the Legion but he'd like to get in on the celebration and he's entitled to do so. He drops around to the local post to put in his application for the medal and comes out of the office a Legionnaire.

A. B. Smith, of New York City, average American citizen of middle age, buys his morning paper on the way to business. In it there is the story of a Legion post that brought order out of chaos in a little Texas oil-boom town. Mr. Smith hitherto had the vaguest idea of what the Legion stood for. Now he understands.

Joe Jones, on his farm in Kansas, lifts his favorite weekly out of the mail box by the gate and sits down on the front porch to see what's up in the world. He finds two columns of news about The American Legion and a picture or so. This is pie for Joe, who belongs to the post in the next town. He spends an interested half hour reading about what other posts are doing and comes across some War Risk Insurance information that is very important to him because he hadn't been able to get to the last two meetings of his post.

And so it goes. Bill Brown, of Kewanee, who joined the Legion; Smith of New York, who found out what the Legion stands for, and Joe Jones, Kansas Legionnaire, whose insurance problem was solved, each represents thousands of persons who are being reached every day in the countrywide publicity sent out by The American Legion News Service.

NEWS of The American Legion now is appearing regularly in more than 4,000 morning, evening and weekly papers because the News Service puts it there. And it is being printed by editors because it is real news about real men. The News Service, in the two months of its existence, has developed into a great agency for placing the activities of the Legion before millions of newspaper readers. Also, it provides THE AMERICAN LEGION WEEKLY with Legion news and features.

The headquarters of the News Service are located at 627 West Forty-third Street, New York. Branch bureaus are in Indianapolis and Washington. To headquarters correspondents appointed in every post of the Legion send the news and gossip of their activities, and from this mountain of "copy" the material is culled for releases to be sent over the country.

Some of these stories are sent out

over the great wire services of the Associated Press, the United Press Association and the International News Service. Others go out through the Newspaper Enterprise Association and other news and picture-distributing syndicates. Still others are mailed direct to the editors of newspapers in every State, and in almost every town that boasts a newspaper. Legion publications also are supplied with news by this service. A special Legion department, two columns long, is provided each week to the smaller newspapers by arrangement with the Western Newspaper Union, which serves 1,000 of these influential local journals.

IT is the aim of The American Legion News Service to reach a newspaper in every town in which there is a post of the Legion in order to provide the people of that town and the Legionnaires with news of the activities of the organization. The direct service is provided without charge to 2,500 newspapers. If you would like to see your home town paper printing this news of the Legion it is simply a matter of asking the editor to apply for "copy" from The American Legion News Service.

To the Legionnaires acting as post correspondents the thanks of the News Service are due. Besides the local publicity they obtain their posts, theirs are the stories, photographs and ideas which go out to the great and the small newspapers of the country from New York headquarters. Out of the mass of stories submitted only a few each week, of course, are selected for instant telegraph and mail distribution, but those few are read by millions. Others go in the weekly news letter, and still others are released once every three weeks in a special page of "plate." Every line that comes into the office is read with a view to publication in THE AMERICAN LEGION WEEKLY.

The efficiency of the News Service depends, of course, upon the support and cooperation it receives from the posts. If your post has not yet appointed a correspondent it is missing an opportunity to help the rest of the Legion and it is overlooking an opportunity to get publicity and attention.

A story for the News Service may come from a post of twenty men in the Arizona desert just as easily as from one of a thousand in New York or San Francisco, and once put out on the Legion News Service it travels from coast to coast. It may come from a man who never had written a line for publication or it may come from a trained reporter. You do not have to be a post correspondent to send in news. Every Legionnaire as likely as not has bottled up in him a crackerjack yarn that the News Service would jump at. If you think you've got one, shoot it along—the News Service will do the rest.

The director of the News Service is Marquis James, of Oklahoma, formerly editor of THE AMERICAN LEGION WEEKLY and later national director of publicity. On the New York staff are James E. Darst, of Missouri, and Steuart M. Emery, of New Jersey. Herbert H. Updegraff, of California, is in charge of the Indianapolis Bureau. The Washington correspondent is J. W. Rixey Smith, of Virginia.

(c) Underwood & Underwood

Amid scenes such as this the Legionnaires of Honolulu wander

NORTH, SOUTH, EAST AND WEST

ALL Americans don't live in America. Some of them are in England, others in France, and still others with bayonets on their rifles are patrolling the bridgehead at Coblenz. The call of country is ever strong in their breasts, but still they must dwell for a time on foreign shores whither the varied job in hand has called them.

Then, too, there are sturdy young Yankees whose business it is to see that American trade is carried to the farthest outposts of their native land—to Alaska, Hawaii, the Philippine Islands and the Isthmus of Panama. And others, filled with the wanderlust, have set themselves up in the Land of the Rising Sun and in China, in Mexico, in Cuba, and in the republics of South America. Wherever you may wander over the face of this terrestrial sphere, above or below the equator or east or west of the meridian, in every land and clime you will find them.

They are the ambassadors of the flag. And many of them fought for the flag at Cantigny, at Château Thierry, at St. Mihiel and in the wire-mazed wilderness of the Argonne. These men are the ones who, now that the war is over, are perpetuating the memories of their days of service at the meetings of the Legion posts that they have formed thousands of miles from home.

Go to Paris and you will find a Legion post in the Rue de l'Elysée. Pick your way through the fog of London and you will stumble on a Legion post there. Cross the Channel again to Brussels and you can drop in on another post meeting. Call a corporal of the guard at Coblenz and he will be, as likely as not, a member of some post. Make your way to shattered Poland and you can shake hands with the war-worn Legionnaires of the Kosciusko Squadron. Move on to the Far East, and in Shanghai, Tokyo, Yokohama, Manila and Cavite a greeting is waiting for you from the men who wear the blue and gold emblem.

STOP off awhile at Hawaii and you will be hailed by buddies of nine posts, and then steer north to Alaska, where thirteen posts from Anchorage to Nome and from Juneau to Fairbanks have a bunk and chow waiting for hiking Legionnaires. And then, if you find Alaska in the throes of winter and the tropics are calling, a Legion welcome is awaiting you in Mexico City; Cristobal, Canal Zone; Santo Domingo or Buenos Aires.

Forty-three of these posts outside the limits of the United States have been formed since the last convention. Their enrollment is in the neighborhood of 12,000. The Paris Post, with a membership of 1,000, is the largest. And it is only one of three posts in France. The others are at Gievres and at La Rochelle.

It is wholly logical that Paris should have a post of the Legion, for this city is the birthplace of the Legion. Here it was in the middle of March, 1919, that officers and enlisted men of all

A. E. F. organizations assembled to draw up the plans for the veterans' organization. It was in September, 1919 —six months after the Paris caucus— that Charles Beale, demobilized A. E. F. veteran, and Barris Katz, who was still in the service, started the machinery of the Paris Post. On Sunday, November 10, 1919, the first meeting of the Post was held.

The Paris Post had its full share of the tribulations which a new organization may expect. Early it lost its original home and got an office in the Elysee Palace Hotel, which was an A. E. F. headquarters during the war. Later it moved to its present quarters in the building of the American Library Association at 10 Rue de l'Elysee. This building was once the home of the Papal legate. Now the Paris Post occupies the entire second floor.

Located in the capital of our ancient ally, the Paris Post has realized that it stands for America and all that the word means. It has declared a principle of strengthening the friendship between the two republics. One of its first works was to provide a memorial to the love of the American soldier for the children of France, by establishing a fund from which yearly prizes will be awarded for the best essay written by any boy or girl in a Paris lycee upon a subject which links the history of France and America.

The Post has conscientiously carried out its obligations to its members and to all former service men. From time to time ex-service men whom Fate has not treated too kindly have been assisted in obtaining employment. At the outset it was not easy to extend this assistance. But American business men were quick to understand that the Legion had a real purpose in Paris and their doors began to open to Legionnaires. Business men were told the names of honorably discharged service men who were seeking work. In the first seven weeks of its operation, the Service Bureau of the Post obtained positions for more than 100 men.

From its own funds the Post has given assistance to ex-service men in urgent need. The loans it has made have been regarded as debts of honor by those who received them. Some of the loans have enabled men to start in business on a small scale. The Post has also aided men who wished to return to America but had insufficient funds. Transportation was provided to a port and the men were helped to obtain concessions for their voyage home. The members of the American colony have co-operated with the Post in lending as-

sistance to former service men who are ill and needy.

For veterans who become entangled in legal difficulties in France because they are more or less unfamiliar with the laws of the country, the Post has its Legal Committee, composed of American lawyers, members of the Post. These lawyers, working with French attorneys, extend to American veterans unusual assistance. The Post does not aid men to evade justice, but its aim is to assist the innocent.

The Women's Auxiliary of the Post now has more than fifty members and new applications are being received daily.

IN England, the land of tea, jam and Woodbines, the London Post, as might be expected, is flourishing. Made up of members from the American Embassy, American Consulates, the U. S. Shipping Board, American Relief Administration, U. S. Army Liquidation Commission and Graves Registration Service, and numbering in its ranks students from Oxford and Cambridge, lawyers, chemists, journalists, engineers, salesmen, valets and chauffeurs, it stands as a representative post of 110 Legionnaires.

One woman is a member of London Post. She is Miss Alice Emerson Findley, who, first with the British and then with the American Army, saw service as a nurse under fire on several of the big fronts. In recognition of her service she holds decorations from Great Britain, France and Belgium, and two stars are on her Victory Ribbon.

London Post considers that it is the first unit of The American Legion in Europe. Beginning in September, 1919, American ex-service men in Great Britain were enrolled in the American War Veterans Association. This association gave place to The American Legion of Europe on October 17, 1919. The Legion of Europe continued until the receipt of a charter from The American Legion in the United States on November 25, 1919. Under the direction of the Post, 2,500 American graves in England and Ireland were decorated on Memorial Day.

A CROSS thousands of miles of ocean from London Post on this side of the Atlantic is another typical unit of The American Legion. In the perpetual summer of tropical America where the narrow strip of the Isthmus of Panama joins together the continents of North and South America, the Department of Panama has been created, with Panama Canal Post at Cristobal, Heights and Cristobal Post at Cristobal, Canal Zone. The men of the Canal volunteered freely for the war, and saw service in all branches of American armies. They were on land and sea, in the air and under the water. They came back with almost every medal and decoration of America and the Allies.

In September, 1919, a few of these veterans met to form a Post of the Legion. One had recently been an aviator in France, another only a few short months before as a lieutenant of engineers had done things in No Man's Land which high British officers said were impossible. A third, after months of volunteer ambulance driving before America entered the war, had won a commission in the French artillery. The Post grew, another Post became neces-

Officers of London Post: left to right, R. L. Bland, finance officer: L. E. Anderson, commander; W. H. A. Coleman, adjutant

sary, and finally a Department Headquarters was chartered.

In July the Canal Legionnaires held their first annual department convention on the Island of Taboga. There on a shelving hillside near an ancient fishing village, within sight of the spot where Vasco Nunez de Balboa in 1513 discovered the Pacific Ocean, they assembled and elected officers for the coming year, adopted amendments to the Department constitution, and arranged to send delegates to the Cleveland convention.

AND in another outpost of Yankeeland the Legionnaires are much awake and stirring. In the Department of Hawaii, which enrolled nearly a thousand members within the first six months, the boys are going strong. There, where the flag waves at the crossroads of the Pacific, the O. D. is plentiful in barracks, and far-flung pickets and the one-time service men and women of the Legion who know soldier as well as civilian life are working steadily to further harmony between the military and civil population. A tremendous military fête and tournament was staged to this end at Honolulu on July 4.

"The complete Americanization of these islands so that they shall be in truth as well as in name an integral part of the United States and a real mission station for the ideals of liberty, democracy and humanity which the fathers builded into the foundations of this republic," is the aim of the Legionnaires of Hawaii as expressed at their convention. Their delegates who left for the Cleveland meeting did so with instructions to vote for the exclusion of Japanese immigrants from the United States.

Paris, London, Panama, Hawaii, Tokyo, Montreal, Brussels, Havana—the Legion spirit in one and all is the same. The list of Departments and posts formed outside the United States in the last year follows:

DEPARTMENT OF ALASKA: Jack Henry Post, Anchorage; Valdez Post, Valdez; Ketchikan Post, Ketchikan; Bradford Post, Juneau; Isaac Evans Post, Seward; Merlin Elmer Parlin Post, Wrangell; John T. Bossi Post, Fort Liscum; John W. Jones Post, Cordova; Nome Post, Nome; DaVidson Post, Haines; Dorman H. Baker Post, Fairbanks; Sitka Post, Sitka; Petersburg Post, Petersburg.

DEPARTMENT OF HAWAII: Honolulu Post, Honolulu; Kauai Post, Lihue, Kauai; Hilo Post, Hilo; Post No. 4, North Kohala; Waialua Post, Waialua, Oahu; Schofield Barracks Post, Schofield Barracks; Col. Elmer J. Wallace Post, Fort Kamehameha; Maui Post, Wailuku, Maui.

DEPARTMENT OF PHILIPPINE ISLANDS: Manila Post, Manila; Lieut. Quentin RooseVelt Post, Manila; CaVite Post, CaVite; C. Perry Rich Post, Fort William McKinley; Philippine Scouts Post, Fort William McKinley.

DEPARTMENT OF CANADA: Yankee Post, Montreal.

DEPARTMENT OF FRANCE: Paris Post, Paris; Loire et Cher Post, GteVres Camp; Standard Post, La Rochelle.

DEPARTMENT OF PANAMA: Panama Canal Post, Balboa Heights; Cristobal Post, Cristobal, Canal Zone.

GERMANY: Amaroc Post, Coblenz.

ENGLAND: London Post, London.

BELGIUM: Brussels Post, Brussels.

POLAND: Kosciusko Post, Warsaw.

JAPAN: Tokyo-Yokohama Post, Tokyo-Yokohama.

CHINA: Gen. Frederick Ward Post, Shanghai.

MEXICO: Tampico Post, Tampico; Mexico City Post, Mexico City.

CUBA: HaVana Post, HaVana.

SANTO DOMINGO: Edward C. Fuller Post, Santo Domingo, R. D.

Miss Alice E. Findley, of London Post

ADAMSON, DOVA W., wants to hear from friends, officers and enlisted men, of the 3d Bn., 59th Inf., or 29th Co., Camp Gordon July Aut. Repl. Draft. Address 1325 W. 37th Place, Los Angeles, Cal.

AVRITT, C. V., formerly 15th Service Co., Fort Leavenworth, write W. S. L., ex-sgt.-maj., 6th. Tr. Bn., Box 309, Salem, Ore.

BAINES, WILLIE R., formerly 104th Ord. Rep. Shop. Information sought by Leo A. Spillane, American Legion, 158 State House, Boston, Mass.

BARROW, ALVIN, formerly Lt., Co. A. 352d Inf., write P. H. Kingmus, 90 Lemon st., Dubuque, Iowa.

BESTANT, HESLIN H., formerly Co. C., 156th Inf., write E. F. Warren, Canton, Miss.

CAMERON, FRANCIS F., formerly 2d Eng., write Harlan L. Shattuck, Glockner, San.; Colorado Springs, Colo.

CAPLAN, SAMUEL J., formerly 51st Inf. M. G. Co., write Donald G. King, 4581 Royal ave., Indianapolis, Ind.

CARTER, PHILIP, 306th Am. Tr., write Martin Farmer, Marshall, Mo.

CLIFF, ELBRIDGE P., formerly Co. B, 133d M. G. Bn. Whereabouts sought for grandmother by Commander, American Legion, Malden, Mass.

CRAUGHAN, VERNIE. Information desired by father, L. H. Craughan, Old Exchange Bldg., Sioux City, Iowa.

CUPERMAN, ISIDOR, Brooklyn, N. Y., write L. Goldstein, Solen, N. D.

DAMON, SAMUEL L., 23d Eng. Information wanted by John Barley, Gen. Del., Palo Alto, Cal.

DOMES, BARNEY, formerly U. S. N., write E. R. Hatfield, 921 Jefferson, Toledo, Ohio.

ELTON, A. S., and others of old 302d Bn., Hq. Co., Tank Corps, write Jay H. Metcalf, 933 Cherry st., Grand Rapids, Mich.

ESTY, ROY T., formerly 104th Co., 8th Marines, Galveston, write Cyril Tapager, Lake Mills, Iowa.

HALFACRE, LEONARD J., U. S. M. C., write Gail L. Speith, 922 Fifth ave., Seattle, Wash.

HILEMAN, FLOSS N. and JESSE C., brothers. Information wanted by sister, Mrs. Dessie Riggs, Box 196, Rawlesburg, W. Va.

HILL, JACK, formerly Magazine Guard, 35th Co., Mare Island, write Cyril Tapager, Lake Mills, Iowa.

HOOVER, G. C. W., Hq. Co., 12th Eng., write C. W. Leavitt, Ex-14th Eng., 601 High st., Dedham, Mass.

JOHNSON, G. Y., C5. C, 47th Inf., write Stuart B. Walther, Y. M. C. A., 215 W. 23d st., New York City, concerning death of Karl Morandi.

JOHNSON, HARRY E., formerly 79th F. A. Supply Co., 36 Falcon st., East Boston, Mass., would like to hear from other members of this outfit.

JOHNSON, WILLIAM, formerly Co. A, 536th Eng., write James F. Dolan, 438 Second st., East Newark, N. J.

KENNEDY, JOHN F., formerly Co. D, 106th Inf., write W. V. Paul, 115 John st., Port Richmond, N. Y.

KING, WILLIAM E., last heard from in Co. A, 8th M. O. R. S., Camp Lee, Va. Information wanted by sister, Mrs. Edward A. Lyon, Lewiston, Idaho.

McHASEN, Cook, formerly Co. F., 2d Eng. Address wanted by Frank S. Summers, Mexico, Mo.

MARTIN, Mech., and MENARD, formerly 3d Bn. Hq., 313th Inf., write Robert F. Jean, Route 3, Salem, N. J.

MEERS, DELBERT A., formerly in S. O. S. Tours, write J. A. Erskine, 1330 Marine Trust Bldg., Buffalo, N. Y.

MOORE, LEO J., 568 Pavone st., Benton Harbor, Mich., wants to hear from buddies of Co. M., 34th Inf.

RANKIN, WALTER A., Q. M. C., formerly Camp Bragg, Fayetteville, N. C., write James D. Grist, Yorkville, S. C.

ROGERS, "MARY," formerly Corp., 90th Div., write Theo. M. Crary, Red Cross, Viroqua, Wis.

SHERWOOD, ARTHUR, Co. K, 327th Inf., not heard from since Sept. 13, 1918. Information wanted by S. D. Schuyler, 207 Schultz Bldg., Columbus, Ohio.

SLOLNICKER, HARRY, formerly 9th Inf. Hq. Co., write Armine Young, Independence, Ore.

SOWDER, CHARLES A., formerly Co. D., 6th Inf., write Anton Kirkemeyer, 270 Chestnut st., Breese, Ill.

TAYLOR, Bty. F, 42d R. A! R., write Aloys Volk, Harvey, N. D.

TEEGARDEN, CABIUS, Co. K, 148th Inf. Information sought by Ben McElfresh, Georgetown, Ohio.

TEN EYECK, JIMMIE, Co. A, 128th Inf., write Theo M. Crary, Red Cross, Viroqua, Wis.

TOMLIN, ROY C., formerly Co. F., 2d Eng. Address wanted by Frank S. Summers, Mexico, Mo.

TUCKER, R., formerly 104th Co., 8th Marines, write Cyril Tapager, Lake Mills, Iowa.

WEAVER, DAVID and LEROY, Co. M., 148th Inf., write Ben McElfresh, Georgetown, Ohio.

WHITMAN, BENJAMIN, Y. M. C. A., St. Oven en Belin, write Eric Gustavson, Scandia, Kans.

WHITWORTH, ROBERT, formerly 70th Co. Marines, write Paul H. Nelins, Fornfelt, Mo.

WOOLEY, PAUL V., formerly in A. E. C. at the Sorbonne, write Henry D. Hopkins, 4057 Drexel ave., Chicago, Ill.

WRAY, GEORGE, formerly of the Prince Frederick William, write John H. Bunning, Hathaway Inn, Deal Beach, N. J.

EVAC. HOSP. No. 27, Annex, Treves—All members are asked to send their present and permanent addresses to Dr. James W. Davis, Statesville, N. C.

23D INF., Co. H.—John R. Phelan, Brown-Potter Apts. Saranac Lake, N. Y., wants to hear from buddies of this outfit.

In the Casualty List

SAGE, JOHN, Co. I, 363D INF.—Relatives may obtain photograph of his grave from Phil Kats, 71 Parker ave., San Francisco, Calif. S. A. R. D., Co. G.—Pvt. Otto Troester died of pneumonia at Camp Morn Hill, Winchester, Eng. Information wanted for relatives by Adjutant, American Legion Post, Guttenberg, Iowa.

5TH MARINES, 2D BN.—Wheatley D. Lewis reported killed in action in October, 1918; later reported missing in action. Information sought by mother, Mrs. L. Lewis, 2033 S. Cecil st., Philadelphia, Pa.

18TH INF., Co. K.—Edward H. Kuhnle killed in action July 28, 1918. Particulars of death and burial and photograph wanted by sister, Mrs. H. F. Huber, 238 31st st., Oakland, Calif.

23D INF.—Pvt. Elmer Hughes last heard from in hospital in France. Information desired by mother, Mrs. Mary Hughes, Carl Junction, Mo.

23D INF., Co. M.—Selva S. Hensley died of wounds at Hospital No. 8, or No. 31 on September 9, 1918. Details wanted by sister, Mrs. A. O, Williams, De Queen, Ark.

28TH INF., Co. K.—William Lehwald reported killed in action on Nov. 7, 1918. Men who were with him at time of death are asked to write to his sister, Miss Martha Lehwald, Route 3, Dayton, Ohio.

28TH INF., Co. M.—Frank R. Matthew wounded Oct. 1, 1918. Whereabouts sought by Mrs. C. C. Matthew, 750 Kelly st., Zanesville, Ohio.

58TH INF., Co. E.—Walter R. Manette died of wounds Oct. 6, 1918. Details wanted by Miss Sarah Monette, 280 Third ave., Duluth, Minn.

60TH INF., Co. C—Members of this outfit who were in action near Cunel, France, on Oct. 14, 1918, are asked to write to Mrs. Marie C. Thune, De Lamere, N. D.

101ST INF., Co. D.—Chester R. Howland reported as having died in B. H. No. 70. Particulars wanted by mother, Mrs. Emma W. Howland, 7 Spring st., Plymouth, Mass.

128TH INF., Co. M.—Daniel Harder killed in action at Cantigny, May 28, 1918. Details desired by brother, Michael Harder, Almyra, Ark.

307TH INF., Co. M.—Ambrose J. Cunningham killed in the Argonne on Oct. 4 or 5, 1918. Particulars wanted by brother, Eugene M. Cunningham, 1646 43d st., Brooklyn, N. Y.

328TH INF., Co. I.—Charles L. Carr killed in Cornay, Meuse, offensive on Oct. 8, 1918. Information wanted by wife, Mrs. Madeline A. Carr, West Newbury, Mass.

FIRST GENERATION HEROES

(Continued from page 12)

rines, is only one of the names on the Medal of Honor roll which show the contribution of the Gaelic clans to American valor. At Blanc Mont Ridge, on October 3, 1918, Kelly ran forward one hundred yards through the American barrage, attacked an enemy machine gun nest, killing the gunner with a grenade and shooting another member of the crew with his pistol, and returned through the barrage with eight prisoners.

Kelly is also still in the Marine Corps. Former service men in any western city may see him one of these days if the "Roving Marines," the special recruiting detachment, should come into their town. They may know him by his ribbon, the one with the blue background spangled with gold stars. And they may verify the identification by his smile—for he is known among his buddies as "Smiling Jack."

Still another Medal of Honor man whose bravery was a reminder that America was repaying what she had obtained from Europe is James C. Dozier, formerly of the 118th Infantry, Thirtieth Division. Although practically all Dozier's life before the war had been spent in his native town of Rock Hill, S. C., his remote ancestors lived in France. And it was fitting that, in addition to winning the Medal of Honor, he was made a Chevalier of the Legion of Honor by the President of the French Republic.

Perhaps several hundred years ago the forbears of Lieutenant Dozier fought in France near the very same town of Montbrehain, where on October 8, 1918, the South Carolina man set

James C. Dozier, who became a hero at Montbrehain in the land of his ancestors, is now a wholesale grocery salesman in South Carolina

an example to a whole army by refusing to be taken to the rear after being wounded in the shoulder, and pressing on at the head of his platoon, to break down enemy opposition. With a sergeant at his side, Lieutenant Dozier attacked a machine gun nest, creeping up on the defenders under intense fire and killing the entire crew with grenades and his pistol. Then he captured a number of prisoners who had taken refuge in a dugout.

South Carolina, his native State, did not overlook the fact that Lieutenant Dozier had distinguished himself. When Lieutenant Dozier last June married the girl who had been waiting for him all during the war, the townspeople presented as a wedding gift a silver service which was inscribed with a tribute to his war heroism. His old company also presented to him a memorial gift, a silver table stand.

The hero of Montbrehain is now staging a single-handed advance in the business field. Although urged by his friends to run for the office of adjutant general of South Carolina, he preferred to join the selling staff of a wholesale grocery company. In this civilian Q. M. C. service he expects to drive ahead to his objective, a store in which he will rank as C. O.

Smiling Jack Kelly, who showed remarkable daring at Blanc Mont, is now with the Roving Marines, getting recruits through the West

[This is the fourth of a series of articles telling what has become of some of the fifty-four living men who won the Congressional Medal of Honor for surpassing courage during the A. E. F.'s battles—EDITOR'S NOTE.]

THE SECOND A. E. F.

(Continued from page 8)

go forth on their own, a-foot by twos and threes, save, perhaps, when some quondam major of Infantry, fulfilling an old promise to show his wife the hill she had heard so much about, hunts up a car and drives her out himself. These all dodge the sight-seeing buses.

Some others succumb occasionally to such alluring ads as "Go Over The Top With A Blue Devil. Every Modern

Comfort." But for the most part, even these confine themselves to the swift trip through Soissons, Rheims and Château-Thierry, which starts from Paris in the morning and lands you back there again in time for a real dinner the next evening. After that, of course, they can say they have covered the battlefields. To be sure, there remains the Argonne and all that, but by this time, they have had enough, most of them. As the man at the tourist agency says, with a shrug: "After all, there's very little variety in ruins."

But your real out-and-out tourist does not take even the shortest of trips. She is too busy in the tempting Paris shops, where, thanks to the rate of exchange, she is able to elbow all the natives out of her way, throw her francs around like a drunken doughboy on pay day night, buy six or seven of everything, and return to America loaded with more gorgeousness than she can possibly sneak past the Customs. This puts her in a bad humor.

"Oh, they just robbed us over there," she complains. "I know the French cheated me at every shop I went into. I often used to tell them frankly I didn't see how they could be so ungrateful after all our boys had done for them. Answer me? But, my dear, what would there be for them to say. They charged me a hundred francs a day for the most appalling room in Paris. Of course, I'll admit they're pretty crowded. Indeed, the dear old place was quite spoiled for me. So many dreadful *tourists.*"

"SOLDIER'S MAIL"

(*Continued from page 6*)

the 2nd I took over the company and we held the line for six days. The Huns attacked us three times and we gave it to them every time and succeeded in holding the lines. I was right in the famous town of Hooge. This line is generally held for two days only, but we held her for six.

The R. C. R.'s are now highly regarded for holding on, and our brigade is now considered the best Canadian brigade out here. I cannot go into details at all, but I tell you it was hell, and I thank God I came through safely. Hope you got my cable worded correctly—"out safely." The regiment had luck which was uncanny. We should have been in the part of the line which was completely wiped out, but changed with another battalion at their request for this tour.

Better keep the following to yourself until I get more details. When I was relieved at Hooge, C. M., K. J. and a lot of boys took over the trench. We left there about 2.30 a. m. and at 8 a. m. the Huns blew two mines into this Coy. of the 28th Battalion. We have no details yet but it is almost certain that very few came back. They may be prisoners, so keep quiet till you know.

The general impression is that the war is in its last stages. Some of the old generals who have been very pessimistic are now absolutely changed. Two months should see something definite.

I expect to be here as long as a month. Had a letter from Dad last night and I was indeed glad to get it. If possible we will finish up our work here soon and then me for *home, home, home.*

My but we were terrible sights when we came from the trenches. None of us had shaved for six days, and we were dirty, and talk about bugs! Think I have some of them yet.

Must stop now and have supper. Will write again very soon. Much, much love to you all. I am still very well and feel top hole.

As ever, your son and brother,
R. B.

R. B. fell in action on October, 1916, during the first battle of the Somme. His body was never found.

The fourth letter is by a doughboy of the A. E. F. It was written just after the battle of St. Mihiel. The writer was killed in action in the Argonne a month and a day later. He was twenty-four years old. He wrote:

With the A. E. F.
Sept. 16, 1918

Dear Cousin:—
Your letter at hand. Was mighty glad to hear from you. You say you hope I came out O. K. after the slight wound I got. I couldn't come out any other way. I am feeling fine and still going strong. Stopped a machine gun bullet with my right arm three or four days ago. Just a slight scratch. I took the A. T. S. shot and had the arm done up at the dressing station and didn't go to the hospital. There was no need of it. If they don't get me any worse than they have so far I won't complain a bit.

We're mighty busy at present and most of us are having the time of our lives. Chasing Huns isn't a very bad job if you use a system. The main trouble is they go so fast that we can't catch up very well. Of course they don't all run.

If they don't lose their breath I guess they will forget to stop when they get to Berlin. We should worry. The faster they run and the sooner they are ready to admit that they are licked, the sooner Uncle Sam will say, "The boats are ready, men; go to them." We don't want that till there is no more Germany but all are working hard to make it happen soon.

After this war is over I hope you can get a chance to take a trip over the war-swept area. It will surely be a liberal education for anyone who can make the trip. Personally, I'll be very well satisfied to stay right in God's own country when I get back to it.

Love to all,
Your cousin, J. C. B.
Cpl. A Co.—U. S. Inf., A. E. F.

So the record stands—and who can show a more sterling chronicle of one hundred percent Americanism?

Regarding Circulation and Editorial Matters

SUBSCRIPTIONS: Annual subscription price, $2.00. Postage free in the United States, its dependencies, and Mexico. Add 50 cents a year postage for Canada, and $1.00 a year for all foreign countries. The annual subscription rate to members of The American Legion is $1.00, payable as National dues through local posts only. Single copies, 10 cents. No subscriptions commenced with back issues.

CHANGES OF ADDRESS: The old as well as the new address must be given with request for change. Legion members should give name and number of post to which they belong. At least two weeks is necessary for a change of address to become effective.

No subscription agents are employed, but regular newsdealers will accept subscriptions from persons other than members of The American Legion.

Address all correspondence to 627 West 43d st., New York City.

EDITORIAL OFFICE: 627 West 43d st., New York City. THE AMERICAN LEGION WEEKLY is always glad to consider articles, jokes and cartoons, and to receive letters and suggestions from its readers. Manuscript should be accompanied by postage and an addressed envelope for return if unaccepted.

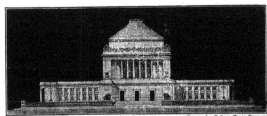

Drawn by Robert Frost Daggett

Architect's drawing of the proposed new home of National Headquarters of The American Legion

A BUILDING FOR HEADQUARTERS

THE first step has been taken to erect a magnificent building to house National Headquarters of The American Legion in Indianapolis. The Indiana State Legislature, at a special session just closed, voted that the Indiana State War Memorial should take the form of a structure for this purpose. The Legislature voted to dedicate to the project a tract of land owned by the State in the center of Indianapolis, 900 feet long by 450 feet wide, and made a tax levy which will yield a little over $3,000,000. The city of Indianapolis also was authorized to associate with the State enterprise a proposal the city had made to include two additional city blocks adjoining the State properties, about 900 feet by 450 feet. These two tracts of land adjoin a city block 450 feet square, making a magnificent plaza, five full city blocks long and one wide, or a total of 2,250 feet long by 450 feet wide. The land is worth about $12,000,000.

The American Legion Headquarters will be built in the center of this plaza. Facing the north end is the new city library and at the south is the new Federal Building. The Legion building is to be constructed under the control of a Board of Trustees appointed by the Governor, one to be selected from each congressional district in the State. All members of this body must be men of The American Legion. No definite figure on the cost of erecting the War Memorial has been set. The appropriation of a little more than $3,000,000 is regarded merely as an evidence of good faith and intent on behalf of Indiana to redeem its pledge adequately and handsomely to house and equip National Headquarters. With the funds in hand, the Board of Trustees, following its organization, will be able to get definite plans and estimates before the next regular session of the Indiana General Assembly in January, 1921, at which time the State is expected to make the appropriation necessary to complete the project.

ARE OUR ORPHANS FORGOTTEN?

AMONG the issues to be brought up at the Cleveland convention is one which is less of an issue than a responsibility. This is the readoption of 3,000 French war orphans and destitute children, former mascots of the A. E. F., who now are facing another winter with every prospect of going cold and hungry.

Once the A. E. F. acted as a provider for them. Now the A. E. F. is back in civilian life, three thousand miles from battlefield and billet, and the suffering children of France to whom Yankee generosity in wartime spelled food and shelter are looking again to their O. D. *parrains* for rescue from their hardships.

The Americanism Commission of the Legion has entered the campaign for readoption of the children on a large scale. Fifteen hundred letters have been sent to State Americanism chairmen, State adjutants, and to the various posts in New Jersey, New York and Connecticut, by Arthur Woods, chairman of the National Americanism Commission, pleading the case of the little unfortunates. Field representatives of the Commission also have been making a personal canvas of the posts in Eastern States, asking a representative of each post to assume personal responsibility for collecting from sources, either inside or outside the Legion, at least $75, the sum required

Andrée Colin, formerly adopted by the 103rd Supply Train, Twenty-eighth Division

for a year's support of an orphan.

Checks for the children's support are being sent to the French Orphan Fund, National Treasurer, American Legion, Indianapolis, Ind. The money is then turned over to the Red Cross, which assigns the children and supervises all expenditures.

THE
Ex-Service
REVIEW

A Digest of News of Interest to the Former Soldier and Sailor

Veterans Speak When Town Fights Hospital

Preparations are being made for the transformation of the Soldiers' Home at Johnson City, Tenn., into a sanitarium of 1,000 beds for tubercular ex-soldiers of the World War, despite protests made by the Johnson City Chamber of Commerce, Kiwanis and Rotary Clubs, the Mayor of the city, and city public health officials. All these, acting together, got the State Public Health Officer of Tennessee to take the matter up with the Government through Senator McKellar of that State.

Senator McKellar merely laid the letters of protest before the Bureau of War Risk Insurance, the Public Health Service and the Vocational Board, without comment. It was not long, however, until he had other letters and resolutions to present. They were from the indignant fathers, mothers, sisters, brothers and friends of the war veterans of Johnson City, who indignantly repudiated the action of their so-called leading citizens and Mayor, and assured the Government that they did not regard these men who had been "broken in health and happiness in defense of their country, including Johnson City" as "lepers or things unclean." "We pledge you," ran one set of resolutions, "that these men whom you send to fight for health, happiness and home among us shall have our most friendly concern, our most neighborly help and our most loyal support in all things."

Venereal Clinics Are Free to All Veterans

Veterans of the World War are entitled to free treatment for venereal disease in the clinics of the Public Health Service, Hugh S. Cumming, Surgeon General of the Service, announces in a statement issued to clear up misunderstandings on the subject caused by a confusion of the "line of duty" provisions of the War Risk Insurance Compensation system.

The treatment of venereal disease by the Public Health Service clinics, located in all the principal cities, is accorded without reference to where, when or how the disease was contracted, the statement says. The only question is whether a person has a venereal disease. If so, its treatment is considered a measure of public welfare and no one is denied the privilege.

Early in the war Congress authorized the Public Health Service to begin a nation-wide campaign to eradicate venereal disease in civilian communities. This was done after investigations showed that syphilis was in a class with cancer and tuberculosis, from a standpoint of number of victims and the gravity of the disease. Other venereal disease was shown to be scarcely less of a menace.

Service men do not have to exhibit discharge papers or service records, and there is no delay or red tape in obtaining treatments. City and state health officers can inform inquirers of the location of the nearest venereal clinic or, inquiries may be made direct to the U. S. Public Health Service, Washington, D. C.

Whisky Is No Longer Medicine in the Navy

After being outlawed by Secretary Daniels long, long ago, one John Barleycorn recently was discovered leading a quiet life in the sick bay of the Navy, but John has now walked the gang plank. The splash of his naval taking off was heard in Washington last week when the Surgeon General of the Navy issued the most drastic restrictions, of distilled spirits, wines or alcoholic preparations. Whisky is stricken from the supply table of the medical department, in the wording of the order. For extreme cases of necessity, ethyl alcohol will be employed instead of whisky, under the new regulations.

All alcoholic preparations now aboard ships are being denatured by the addition of substances which make them unsuitable as beverages. They are being placed in containers labeled, "Dangerous to Drink."

State Party Favors Compensation— Passage of a four-fold national compensation law to aid veterans of the World War is recommended in the state platform of the Republican Party of Missouri, adopted August 31. In part, the plank on this subject says: "While the men who were with the colors, whether injured or not, can never be paid for their services, we believe that insofar as possible, a grateful nation should adjust their compensation to help in some measure to equalize the financial losses which they sustained. To that end, we recommend to the favorable action of the United States Senate the bill which passed the House and which was framed largely along lines recommended by The American Legion."

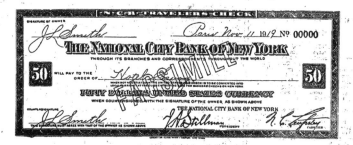

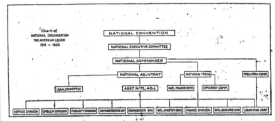

HOW THE LEGION'S G. H. Q. OPERATES

THE above chart is designed to
show the organization of National Headquarters of The
American Legion. At present the
duties of the publicity division are being absorbed by The American Legion
News Service, which operates in con-
junction with THE AMERICAN LEGION
WEEKLY.

In detail the duties of the eight other
divisions of National Headquarters are
as follows:

SERVICE DIVISION: Expediting settlement
of compensation, vocational training, medical,
and hospital claims, reinstating and converting
insurance, handling of pay claims, establishing
service offices in Departments and posts, perfecting liaison between Government bureaus
and Legion agencies, issuing bulletins and
supplying certain kinds of information for publicity purposes.

EMBLEM DIVISION: The protection of pat-
ent rights, the designing, purchasing, advertising, selling and distributing of Legion insignia and other articles, such as buttons,
official jewelry, ceremonial badges, Legion
flags, membership cards and cases, grave
markers, souvenirs, auxiliary emblems, etc.

PUBLICITY DIVISION: Functions absorbed
by American Legion News Service since draft-
ing of above diagram: Gathers, writes and
distributes news and news-pictures of Legion
interest to 4,000 newspapers in all States;
gathers Legion news for AMERICAN LEGION
WEEKLY and other Legion publications; pre-
pares special articles for magazines, etc.;
writes bulletins, pamphlets, statements of
Legion policy, etc.; devises means for keeping
Legion in the news and before the public.

ADMINISTRATIVE DIVISION: The co-ordina-
tion and administration of National Head-

quarters, handling incoming and outgoing mail;
directing stenographic and multiform printing forces, operating general files and super-
vising employment.

ORGANIZATION DIVISION: The formation of
new posts and departments and the development of existing ones. Activities include fur-
nishing official interpretations of policy, surveying conditions, outlining methods and
plans, providing official forms, issuing char-
ters, compiling statistics, operating speakers'
bureau, preparing special programs, liaison
between departments, issuing bulletins and
pamphlets and supplying information to the
Publicity Division and the American Legion
News Service.

NATIONAL AMERICANISM COMMISSION: Ad-
ministering an educational system for combat-
ting un-American activities, tendencies and
propaganda, educating the immigrant and
alien resident, educating the general public in
American ideals and principles of Government
and fostering the teaching of Americanism in
the schools.

FINANCE DIVISION: The receiving and dis-
bursing of all funds and the administration of
the general financial policy. This division col-
lects national dues from departments, handles
special donations, such as the French War
Orphan Fund and Graves Decorating Fund.

THE NATIONAL LEGISLATIVE COMMITTEE:
Works for the passage of approved legislation,
acts as counsel in litigation and obtains special
information. The committee maintains contact with Congress, state legislatures, department legislative committees, co-ordinates post
efforts in support of legislation and advises on
proposed legislation.

LEGION PUBLISHING CORPORATION: Directs
publication of THE AMERICAN LEGION WEEKLY
for the furthering of Legion policies, distribution of official information and exposition of
special subjects; and the American Legion
News Service.

"BOOKS FOR EVERYBODY"

A "BOOKS FOR EVERYBODY" effort is now being conducted by the
American Library Association,
which put some two million books in the
hands of American soldiers and sailors,
both at home and overseas, during the
war and the Armistice period. The
goal of the effort is a fund of two
million dollars. With this sum the
American Library Association hopes to
reach many of the sixty million people
in the United States who are at present
without library facilities. Especial interest attaches to the effort because the
organization has assumed the responsibility of providing books for the soldiers who lost their eyesight in the war.

Books have advanced in price no less
than most other necessities, so that the
Association's endeavor to get library
replacements—for books become ready
casualties after a hard campaign or
two—not to mention the greatly increased cost of administrative expenses,
have added considerably to its financial
burden. The address of the Association
is 24 West Thirty-ninth street, New
York City.

A face casualty with an A. L. A. book

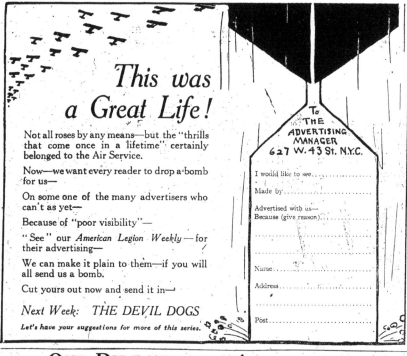

This was a Great Life!

Not all roses by any means—but the "thrills that come once in a lifetime" certainly belonged to the Air Service.

Now—we want every reader to drop a bomb for us—

On some one of the many advertisers who can't as yet—

Because of "poor visibility"—

"See" our *American Legion Weekly* — for their advertising—

We can make it plain to them—if you will all send us a bomb.

Cut yours out now and send it in—

Next Week: THE DEVIL DOGS

Let's have your suggestions for more of this series.

To THE ADVERTISING MANAGER 627 W. 43 St. N.Y.C.

I would like to see................

Made by.......................

Advertised with us—
Because (give reason).............

Name.....................

Address.....................

Post.......................

OUR DIRECTORY of ADVERTISERS

These Advertisers support us—Let's reciprocate. And tell them so by saying, when you write—"I saw your ad. in our AMERICAN LEGION WEEKLY." Or tell the same thing to the salesman from whom you buy their products.

We do not knowingly accept false or fraudulent advertising, or any advertising of an objectionable nature. See "Our Platform," issue of February 6, 1920. Readers are requested to promptly report any failure on the part of an advertiser to make good any representation contained in an advertisement in THE AMERICAN LEGION WEEKLY.

Advertising rates: $3.00 per agate line. Smallest copy accepted, 14 lines (1 inch.)

THE ADVERTISING MANAGER, 627 West 43d Street, N. Y. City.

Lightning Source UK Ltd.
Milton Keynes UK
UKHW010607120219

337137UK00007B/1545/P